THE CHALLENGE
OF
PARENTHOOD

THE CHALLENGE OF PARENTHOOD

Robin MacKellar

Bridge-Logos *Publishers*

North Brunswick, NJ

The Challenge of Parenthood
by Robin MacKellar
ISBN: 088270-7264
Library of Congress Catalog Card Number: Pending
Copyright © 1997 by Bridge-Logos Publishers

Published by:
Bridge-Logos *Publishers*
North Brunswick Corporate Center
1300 Airport Road, Suite E
North Brunswick, NJ 08902-1700

Dedication

This book is dedicated to my Lord Jesus, that the glory of what He has done in our family be known and acknowledged. To Him be all the glory, thanks, and praise.

It is also dedicated to my family—my husband, Michael; our sons, Duncan and Cam; our daughter, Maggie; and our son-in-law, Mike. Without their permission to share some of the treasures of their hearts, this book could not have been written.

Acknowledgments and Thanks

To Rev. Noel and Phyl Gibson for their encouragement, prayers, and love.

To Malcolm Thiesfield and Pastor Glenn Feehan for their encouragement and practical help.

To Bridge-Logos Publishers—thanks to Guy Morrell for his faith in this book, and Harold Chadwick for editing the text.

And to my prayer partners—Pam, Betty, and Edna (Sydney), Sylvie and Chris (Melbourne), and Sandra (Mudgeeraba).

Table of Contents

Introduction

Therefore every teacher of the law who has been instructed about the kingdom of heaven is like the owner of a house who brings out of his storeroom new treasures as well as old.

(Matthew 13:52)

Four years ago, a group of young mothers at *All Saints Anglican Church* at Balgowlah asked me to give a talk at their morning meeting. As I sought the Lord on what He wanted me to talk about, there came flooding into my mind what are now the chapter titles of this book. I wrote them down as they came to me, gave the talk, and thought no more about them. Several days later, however, that still, small, voice quite clearly said, "Those headings I gave you for that talk—they're really chapters of a book." That was all the urging I needed, and I immediately started writing out of my "storeroom of new treasures as well as old."

In my "storehouse" are those things I've learned about our great God while listening to teachings, reading the

Scriptures, talking and praying with friends, and—the most incredible treasure of all—communicating with the living God, who is Jesus Christ. The *old* treasures are those things that were learned from people I've known, and people in the Scriptures. The *new* treasures are those things received from the Lord while praying for and with our children.

Through prayers and instructing them from the Word of God, I've learned that our children—and grandchildren—can come to understand that they have indeed been "predestined" to be adopted as sons and daughters of God through His Son, our Lord Jesus Christ (Ephesians 1:5), and that they can develop an intimate, personal, relationship with Him. God has no grandchildren, however, and we must not assume that salvation will automatically happen to our children just because we ourselves have come to know Christ.

This book has come out of my experiences, and has been written to share with you the things I've learned about spiritual parenting, in the hope that it will help you to guide *your* children to their eternal destiny in Christ. It goes forth with my prayers.

Robin MacKellar
Balgowlah Heights, Australia
1996

1

The Christian Parent

For you created my inmost being; you knit me together in my mother's womb.

I praise you because I am fearfully and wonderfully made; your works are wonderful, I know that full well.

My frame was not hidden from you when I was made in the secret place. When I was woven together in the depths of the earth,

your eyes saw my unformed body. All the days ordained for me were written in your book before one of them came to be.

(Psalm 139:13-16)

The door to my hospital room burst open, and the light was abruptly switched on. The cheerful voice of the nurse urged me to force my sleep-drenched body awake. "It's 5 A.M. feed time. I'll be back to check on you later." She left as fast as she came in, and I sat staring at the cocoon-like shape in the stainless steel trolley she had abandoned in the middle of the room.

My baby! My son. So unfamiliar, and yet not. We'd been together nine long months. I picked him up gingerly, amazed at his cries—so much noise and energy coming from one tiny body. Will he burst? He was quiet and drinking, and it seemed my life flowed into him from my breast. His tiny fingers found one of mine and grasped it tightly. I gazed at this wonder of creation—tiny fingernails, shell-like ears, and a funny little nose breathing furiously.

What will you be like in 5 years, 10 years, 15, 20?

Is it possible your hand will grow larger, stronger, rougher than mine?

What has life in store for you, what joys, what sorrows?

You are "indeed fearfully and wonderfully made!"

Do all parents feel like this—ridiculously proud, panicky, excited, scared?

What sort of parents will we be?

It isn't hard to put myself back in that hospital bed twenty-four years ago. I remember my search for knowledge that would make me the perfect parent, one who would make all the currently right choices in diet, discipline, clothing, schooling. Looking back, I see that my whole emphasis was on bringing our children to intellectual and physical maturity, while virtually ignoring their spirituality.

C. S. Lewis wrote about the God-made vacuum in each of us, a vacuum that needs to be filled with God, our Father and Creator, sustainer and redeemer, if we are ever to function as we are designed to do, and if we are to have that inner peace "which the world cannot give." As I look back, I recognize the things I put into my vacuum in the hope of feeling fulfilled and worthy.

There was an endless procession of them—endless activities while growing up, leaving home, getting a job, going overseas, getting married, having children.

Eight years after that day in the hospital, I came face to face with the reality that because of Jesus Christ's death on the Cross for me, I could know, communicate with, and eventually love my heavenly Father. I began to mature spiritually. My stunted spiritual body began to blossom and flourish. I began to understand God's purpose for my life. I began to live in God's truth and to know a glorious freedom. Something written by Selwyn Hughes about what we really are helped immensely:

> The Bible says that there are three parts to our being—spirit, soul, and body (1 Thessalonians 5:23). The spirit is the center of our personality, the motivating point of our whole being. The soul is that part of us which contains our mind (or thoughts and memories), our feelings (or emotions), and our will (our decisions).[1]

It's our spirit, therefore, when indwelt by the Holy Spirit, by our invitation and as an act of our will, that motivates our personality—our mind, thoughts, feelings, emotions, and decisions.

In other words, it's really our spirit that is the most important part of our being. It's our spirit that is eternal and lives forever. When our body stops functioning and we die physically, our spirit lives on, and we live spiritually forever, either with God in heaven or without Him in hell. Therefore, we should give even more emphasis and recognition—along with body and soul— to the fact that our children have spirits that need to be educated, nurtured, protected, strengthened, and fed. In my own life , the emphasis on physical and mental education was expensive and reasonably effective, but spiritual education was neglected. I knew practically nothing about spiritual matters, and had precious little understanding or awareness of my spirit. I remember as a child questioning my Christian teachers about the burning bush (Exodus 3:2) that was pictured on our school badges, and was told it was "just the sun shining on a bush in autumn—just a figure of speech."

No talk about miracles.

No talk about a living God who reveals himself to his people, whom He loves and yearns for, and grieves over.

No talk of God the Son, who died for us so we could know the Father.

No talk of God the Holy Spirit, who longed to communicate with our spirit.

Without question, such an explanation can quench and squash a child's spirit, which might gloriously respond to an explanation of truth. Something like: "This burning bush is the beginning of the most wonderful story of the Old Testament. God Himself came down from Heaven and called to Moses from the burning bush (Exodus 3:4). He told Moses how He knew all about the miserable life his people were living in Egypt and how He had heard their cries to Him for help (Exodus 3:7). He told Moses He had a plan to rescue them and take them to a good land with food and space and freedom (Exodus 3:8). He told Moses that He would lead his people out of Egypt by mighty miracles (Exodus 3:20).

How inspiring it would have been if we could have talked about the "flames of fire," and looked up other

Bible references about God coming down as fire. We could also have talked about how Jesus came years later to do exactly the same thing—to rescue us and bring us to a place of freedom, and we could have read about the "tongues of fire" at Pentecost (Acts 2:3). We could have sat and read and discussed all these things that stir and feed a child's spirit, but we live in a society that, generally speaking, "will go to church, yes, but they won't really believe [or speak about] anything they hear" (2 Timothy 3:5, TLB).

Jesus tells us that He is the source of life. He said, "whoever drinks the water I give him will never thirst. Indeed, the water I give him will become in him a spring of water welling up to eternal life" (John 4:14), and, "I am the living bread that came down from Heaven. If anyone eats of this bread, he will live forever" (John 6:51). This is indeed the food and provision of the Promised Land in the Old Testament. Our "promised land" is Christ! He is the living bread and water of the New Covenant.

Just as our children hunger and thirst in their bodies and their minds, so do they hunger and thirst for spiritual truth. As Christian parents and grandparents, we should be excited about the privilege and opportunities of bringing our children into a relationship with the living God through Jesus Christ. Growing with our children in spiritual maturity can be the most challenging and rewarding achievement of our lives. It's exciting and thrilling to lead children into revelation and truth. Jesus tells us to "go and make disciples . . . baptizing them in the name of the Father and of the Son and of the Holy Spirit, and teaching them to obey everything I have commanded you" (Matthew 28:19-20). Our own children

5

are to be our primary disciples. They are entrusted to us by God. We are to be a demonstration to them of how their Father in heaven loves them. We are to bring them from a point of total dependence on us, their earthly parents, to a total dependence on God, their heavenly Father. Christian parenting is discipling and equipping our children for their lives as sons and daughters of the King of kings in His Kingdom. Here is what Ranald Macaulay and Jerram Barrs said in their book, *Christianity With A Human Face:*

> The independence of the child should be a goal to which the parents aim. And it should be fostered deliberately so that with each succeeding year, quietly and perhaps imperceptibly because of its gradualness, the child moves from being under the parents to being alongside them. The Bible gives no age at which this is to be achieved, but it is clearly the whole intention of the parent/child relationship. The parents are to view themselves only as in loco parente, that is, in the place of the parenthood of God. This is what should be uppermost in their minds. In the sense of having their children dependent on them, they are parents for only a short period. God alone is the child's permanent parent. Therefore, they are to aim at withdrawing from their position of authority.[2]

We're talking about *spiritual* independence. Young people may be spiritually independent of their parents at a much earlier age than that at which they're financially independent. For example, when our 15 year old son, Cam, came home from being away with a group of young men from our Church, it was obvious he had reached a new depth in his relationship with his heavenly Father. He described it as "now owning my own faith," and not being dependent anymore on his parents' faith.

I was excited about Cam *owning his own faith,* and there are no better words for describing what it means for children to be spiritually independent from their parents. For children there is no *right age* for spiritual maturity—too many factors determine the age when they become independent. Although it may be a dramatic and sudden moment when they discover that they own their own faith, normally it doesn't result in an instant cut-off in communicating with their parents about spiritual matters. It is, however, a time where children know with an inner knowing that their heavenly Father is both able and willing to meet all their needs. It's an experience of God working directly in their lives without the help of parents, friends, or church workers. Only when we've experienced an intimacy with God on our own, can we launch off in our own faith—and be certain that God will guide us, inspire us, teach us, heal us, love us and empower us.

The LORD told Jeremiah, "Before I formed you in the womb I knew you" (Jeremiah 1:5). If the LORD so knew Jeremiah, then it stands to reason that He knew each one of us before we were "formed in the womb," and that's why small children instinctively know the truth of God when they hear it. They have a hunger for spiritual things. They love the things of His creation—sun, stars, rain, flowers, birds, animals. Because they're not yet operating on a rational level, they react intuitively rather than by rational thought processes, and are open to absorbing the things of God's Spirit.

And what do we do as a society? We spend vast amounts of money, time, and effort educating our children's minds, and training and building up their bodies while giving scant attention to their spirits. Sadly, we leave out the most exciting part of parenting in pursuit of worldly goals, when the Scriptures tell us to do just the opposite.

> *Do not love the world or anything in the world. If anyone loves the world, the love of the Father is not in him.*
>
> *For everything in the world—the cravings of sinful man, the lust of his eyes and the boasting of what he has and does—comes not from the Father but from the world.*
>
> *The world and its desires pass away, but the man who does the will of God lives forever.*
> (1 John 2:15-17)

Jesus told his disciples that unless they were converted and became like little children, they would never enter the kingdom. (Matthew 18:3.) I had always assumed that Jesus meant that we are to be trustful and childlike. But Tom Marshall, in his book, *Free Indeed,* has a different interpretation—one that re-enforces what I've said about children being spiritually aware and operating primarily by instinct or intuition:

> I was never very satisfied with the usual interpretations given to this passage—for example, that we are to be become humble and trusting as little children. I know some children that are not a bit humble and who wouldn't trust you as far as they could see you on a dark night! I do not think the real thrust of what Jesus meant was that at all.

If you go into a home where there is a little toddler, he has you summed up in about fifteen seconds flat! He does it intuitively because he doesn't have much intellectual data about you—and anyway he probably wouldn't understand it! He makes up his mind about you solely on the basis of what his spirit tells him. The interesting thing about a little child is that he goes one hundred percent along with what his intuition tells him. If he decides he doesn't like you, you can't get near him. You may be wreathed in smiles and laden with goodies, but nothing will get him out from behind his mother's skirts or from under the kitchen table. On the other hand, if he decides he does like you, you can't get rid of him. He'll be all over you, sticky fingers and all; and if you won't let him put his half-eaten toffee in your mouth he'll poke it up your nose or in your left ear, so greatly does he want to share with you everything he has.[3]

From this we can see that unless we're willing, like children, to trust the divine knowledge we receive in our spirit, we'll never understand the ways of the kingdom of God.

We need to encourage our children to operate in the supernatural in a natural way. As a friend of mine puts it—to be naturally supernatural and supernaturally natural. The Lord will teach us much through our children if we'll listen and respect them in spiritual matters. We also need to be extremely discerning ourselves. It's our privilege, as Christian parents, to guide our children toward their heavenly Father in every situation they face, and to partner with them in growing more like Jesus.

Our children need to see, through us, that the Bible is a glorious love story—a love story of God the Father yearning for and wooing His children to Himself. Jesus is our model for showing forth the Father's love to our children. Christianity is not a set of rules and rituals, but a relationship of love, trust, obedience, and hope.

Parenting is also like that. The emphasis should be on developing a relationship between parent and child based on love, trust, and respect, rather than on the acquisition and application of parenting skills. With a good relationship between parent and child, discipline will not be a major problem.

Of this we can be sure—the Lord loves our children more than we can ourselves and, through our prayers, He will continue to woo them and yearn for them. Jesus spoke of this yearning in His lament for Jerusalem:

> *O Jerusalem, Jerusalem, you who kill the prophets and stone those sent to you, how often I have longed to gather your children together, as a hen gathers her chicks under her wings, but you were not willing.*
>
> (Matthew 23:37)

Here is the nurturing, aching, heart of God yearning for His people, and longing for them to turn to Him and find safety under His wings. He will not give up on us—or on our children!

2

Your Children's Heritage

You shall not make for yourself an idol in the form of anything in heaven above or on the earth beneath or in the waters below.

You shall not bow down to them or worship them; for I, the LORD your God, am a jealous God, punishing the children for the sin of the fathers to the third and fourth generation of those who hate me,

but showing love to a thousand generations of those who love me and keep my commandments.

(Exodus 20:4-6)

Do not be deceived: God cannot be mocked. A man reaps what he sows.

(Galatians 6:7)

When a baby is expected in a family, our natural response is to provide the best we can afford. In whatever way we are able to provide, our desire is for the best as an expression of our welcome to this new member of our family.

It's also usually a great family time. If it's the first child, it's a time when the dynamics of relationships change. A wife suddenly becomes a mother, and a husband becomes a father. There are grandmothers, grandfathers, aunts, and uncles—each with a new title and role. There's talk of names, family names, and maybe even christening robes that were handed down. Other things are handed down—treasures hidden away for years waiting for the arrival of "my granddaughter"—jewelry, books, clothes, ornaments. Photos are unearthed and exclaimed over: "she's the image of Aunt Jean," or "he's got great-grandfather's nose." We are wondrously aware of the continuity of our family—one generation following on from the one before—an ongoing thread woven in and out, running through us and on into time.

As we look forward, we do so with expectancy, hopes, and fears for the next generation.

But somewhere in all this reverie of passing on traditions, names, possessions, we've lost track of our spiritual inheritance. We're so concerned about our worldly inheritance, that we ignore our spiritual inheritance. We don't consider whether there are things sown in our family's lives, in our own lives, that will bear bad fruit and not the fruit of the Holy Spirit. God brought His chosen people out of Egypt and spent forty years encouraging, discipling, urging, and commanding them to be set apart, not to intermarry, and not to follow other gods (Deuteronomy 6:14 and 7:3). He continuously promised them blessing, freedom, and a wonderful inheritance if only they would follow him.

Oh, that their hearts would be inclined to fear me and keep all my commands always, so that it might go well with them and their children forever!

(Deuteronomy 5:29)

So be careful to do what the LORD your God has commanded you; do not turn aside to the right or to the left.

Walk in all the way that the LORD your God has commanded you, so that you may live and prosper and prolong your days in the land that you will possess.

(Deuteronomy 5:32-33)

God says exactly the same thing to us today:

But you are a chosen people, a royal priesthood, a holy nation, a people belonging to God, that you may declare the praises of him who called you out of darkness into his wonderful light.

Once you were not a people, but now you are the people of God; once you had not received mercy, but now you have received mercy.

(1 Peter 2:9-10)

So it follows that if we're "a people belonging to God," we need to delivered from our sinful inheritance, just as the Israelites were—and we can be, because of Jesus. Some of us have parts of our inheritance that are ungodly. We may have inherited allegiance to other gods, practices of witchcraft and occult, freemasonry, New

Age, or false religions. We ourselves may have been promiscuous, adulterous, slaves of addiction to alcohol or drugs. Or we may have inherited grandfather's dreadful anger or fear, or grandmother's sense of rejection and worthlessness. The list is endless—materialism; homosexual tendencies; sexual lust; or lust for power, money, clothes, or possessions.

If we look at the passage from Exodus 20:4-6, we see that God desires and promises to show his love down through a thousand generations. It's obvious, then, that God made this law of inheritance in order for us to reap the good things—the blessings down through the generations. Here God is explaining His law of sowing and reaping, first demonstrated in Genesis when Adam and Eve reap what they sowed—the fruit of their sin (Genesis 3:16-19).

Now God doesn't reverse His laws in order to rescue us if we choose to abuse them. He doesn't reverse the physical law of gravity if a person chooses to jump out of a ten story window. Laws are set up for our good, and God leaves us to cope with the consequences of our abuse of His laws. So also He doesn't reverse the spiritual law of sowing and reaping when we—or our parents, grandparents, or great-grandparents—choose to abuse it by sinning. Saint Paul says, "Do not be deceived: God cannot be mocked. A man reaps what he sows" (Galatians 6:7). Only through Jesus Christ, the ultimate sacrifice, can this law be reversed.

Bearing in mind that Jesus told us that He did not come to abolish the Law, but to fulfill it, we need to look at the New Testament teaching of the consequences of idolatry and sin in our lives and those of our children.

Jesus' teaching on the cost of being a disciple in Luke 14:25-35 may seem a little extreme to some. But there can be no compromise. There's no room for idolatry, whether it be relationships, material possessions, jobs, hobbies, or interests. Unless we love our Lord more than all these things, and would be willing to give them up if He told us to, we *cannot* be His disciples.

If we understand His teaching and the consequences of either our obedience and desire to follow it, or our disobedience and rebellion to it, then we will more fully understand Exodus 20:4-6 and the law of sowing and reaping. We'll also understand more fully the need to hand down to our children and grandchildren a godly inheritance of blessing, love, faithfulness, holiness, and obedience. We're often quick to blame outside circumstances, Satan, and even God Himself, when things go wrong rather than looking to our own lives, and those of our forefathers, for a possible explanation. All too often, our legacy to our children is one of a careless and apathetic approach to holiness, unbelief in the promises of God and who He really is, and a worship of man-made things.

When I invited Jesus to be Lord of my life, it was suggested that I could have been sinning by running my life my own way without looking to God for help and direction. That statement amazed me! I considered myself a moral person, one who had made a good attempt at following the ten commandments, though I had trouble with the thought of loving an unseen God with all my heart, soul, mind and strength. I had no conviction of my own sin before God, but only a concept of sin in relation to society, which, of course, is entirely different to God's

15

concept of sin. Consequently, I never realized that it was possible to pass on to my children anything other than a physical inheritance. I was totally unaware that a spiritual inheritance could be passed on to them that would make them vulnerable to such things as unbelief, pride, witchcraft, promiscuity. Thankfully, despite the mess my life had been in, God is transforming me more each day to be like Jesus, and it is as I am obedient to Him, and through my prayer life, that He is able to bless our children. In other words, they are now inheriting a blessing from my life rather than a curse.

When we hold our babies in our arms, and our thoughts turn to the physical and material inheritance we have planned for them, we need to be mindful of the spiritual inheritance we are handing on to them. Certainly they are cut off from sins that we've committed before their conception, or which have been committed by our ancestors, but which have been confessed and forgiven and the bondage broken by the power of our Lord Jesus Christ. Many parents, however, haven't dealt with sins committed before their marriage, and their children seem often to inherit the tendency to sin in those same areas—or, in other words, they inherit the legal access Satan has to their parents, and so they are easy prey when temptation comes.

For instance, there is a tendency for young Christian couples who don't want to sin by having a sexual relationship before they marry, to marry in order to satisfy their sexual desires. A good sexual relationship in marriage is a wonderful gift from God, and is to be enjoyed to the full. When a marriage is based on these sexual desires, however, what often happens is that the couple deals with a problem of lust by marrying, and hopes they won't have a problem anymore.

They may well keep their problem under control in this way, and think that they no longer have a problem in controlling their lustful desires and thoughts, because these thoughts and desires are, hopefully, directed toward their partner. There is a strong possibility, however, that their children will inherit either a lustful spirit, or a strong tendency to commit sexual sins. Parents of such children will be greatly alarmed at their sexual interests, even when quite young, and will blame it on society, the children's friends, the media, books, etc., when all the time they should be looking at their own lives, and the sinful attitudes and desires they themselves sowed in their children.

We're living in a society where it has become quite normal and publicly acceptable for a couple to live together before marriage, or even not to marry at all. Our young people need to be encouraged to believe that the Lord will honor their desire not to commit sexual sins, but we also need to pray for them and give them a pure inheritance in this area.

God's desire to bless his people is strongly emphasized right through the Old Testament. The conditional blessing of the Old Testament is obedience, and the conditional blessing of the New Testament is also obedience in the form of our submission to the Lordship of Jesus. The desire of God is the same, yesterday, today, and tomorrow—to love and bless us. Moses tells the Israelites to "Know therefore that the LORD your God is God; he is the faithful God, keeping his covenant of love to a thousand generations of those who love him and keep his commands" (Deuteronomy 7:9).

Timothy was blessed because of the faithfulness of his mother and grandmother. Paul says that their "sincere

17

faith" lived also in Timothy (2 Timothy 1:5). Timothy was obedient and reaped the blessing. A careful reading of Deuteronomy 28 will give greater understanding of the law of sowing and reaping, and Derek Prince's teaching on this subject is extremely helpful, particularly his book, *Blessing or Curse - You Can Choose!*[4]

The patterns of generational sin in the Old Testament are interesting and convincing to trace. A curse on King David follows his adultery with Bathsheba and the murder of her husband (2 Samuel 11). Nathan the prophet tells David, "But because by doing this you have made the enemies of the Lord show utter contempt, the son born to you will die. . . . On the seventh day the child died" (2 Samuel 12:14, 18).

In the story of Jacob we can see the thread of deception weaving down into each generation. At the suggestion of his mother, Rebekah, and with her help, Jacob deceives his father, Isaac, and obtains the fatherly blessing that Isaac had intended to give to Esau (Genesis 27). Jacob is subsequently deceived by his father-in-law, Laban, when he unknowingly marries Leah instead of Rachel as Laban had promised (Genesis 29:15-30). Subsequently Rachel, his favored wife, deceives her father and her husband by stealing her father's household gods (Genesis 31:19). Unaware of this, and confronted with the theft by Laban, Joseph unwittingly curses his wife, Rachel, when he says to Laban, "But if you find anyone who has your gods, he shall not live" (Genesis 31:32). Rachel dies when giving birth to Benjamin (Genesis 35:18).

Later in the story, Jacob is deceived by his own sons into believing his precious son Joseph was dead (Genesis 37:12-36). It is a confirmation of the loving nature of

God that, in spite of this chain of deception, Joseph—because of his faithfulness and obedience to God—is able to rescue his people from famine, and bring them to a place of great provision. Joseph tells his brothers, "You intended to harm me, but God intended it for good to accomplish what is now being done, the saving of many lives" (Genesis 50:20).

There are other instances in the Old Testament of recurring generational sin. Abraham twice lies about his relationship with Sarah, calling her his sister (Genesis 12:12-13, 20:2). Isaac does exactly the same thing, saying of his wife, Rebekah, "She is my sister," for fear of being killed (Genesis 26:7). Because both these men, Abraham and Isaac, were part of the anointed line of inheritance to Jesus, their lies were unnecessary. God would have protected them if they had only trusted in Him, but don't we display the exact same lack of trust in our own lives? With God nothing is impossible, except maybe when we take matters into our own hands and try and *play God* ourselves.

Spiritual law is meticulously legal. Satan has legal access into many families through generational sin, and we are all too often oblivious of it. If he has legal right through a person's sinful inheritance, to influence lives of children, he will use every tiny crack or foothold he can.

Jesus was able to declare that the devil had no part of Him. Jesus was sinless with a Godly inheritance that was holy and pure, so Satan had no legal right to control Him. Satan could and did tempt Jesus, but he was never able to influence or control Him. Because of what Jesus has done for you and me and our families on the Cross, we can be set free of generational sin and curses. "Christ redeemed us from the curse of the law by becoming a curse for us, for it is written: Cursed is everyone who is hung on a tree" (Galatians 3:13).

We only have to come to God in prayer in the name of his precious son Jesus, empowered with the authority that is ours as his sons and daughters, and ask to be set free from generational sin and curses. Jesus has already died for our sin and for the curse on our lives. All we have to do is claim it!

To taken an example of generational sin from my own life—our son, Cam, was conceived and carried in fear. Our first son, Duncan, had at the time been diagnosed as having a severe mental disability, and we had no real idea of what the future would hold for him. There seemed no obvious medical reason why this should happen again, but the fear was certainly on everyone's mind, not the least on mine and that of our family, friends, and doctors. Had I been a Christian and understood that fear is a sin that needs to be confessed and replaced by faith, and had I realized that Jesus was constantly telling his followers not to fear, I would not have been so consumed by it. But when I became pregnant, I was filled with fear. My mother told me that I aged ten years in nine months.

The fear began to manifest in Cam at an early age, his spirit being obviously unprotected by the Holy Spirit. Whenever he was put in a situation of uncertainty or stress, he would become quiet and complain of headaches. At the age of six, he was diagnosed as having severe migraine headaches, and would suffer with blind spots in his vision and vomiting that often lasted for days, or until the uncertainty or stress was alleviated. By this time I was a Christian, and so I asked the Lord to show me the cause of these headaches. Immediately I remembered the fear and stress while carrying Cam. After asking the Lord to forgive me, I asked Cam to forgive me, and together we asked for healing. The headaches stopped. Some ten years later, Cam casually told me, "You know, I can't remember the last time I was really scared of anything. Maybe you over-did it."

I have prayed for children who have been conceived in adulterous relationships. Such children often develop unusual interest in sex, are usually rejected if they don't live with both parents, and are often deceitful because adultery always leads to deception. These children have had their foundations in the sand, like the house that Jesus talked about in Matthew 7:24-27. They have an ungodly inheritance of some or all of the following: lust, rejection, fear of abandonment, lying, and a sense of unworthiness. When these strongholds are broken over their lives, and they have been cleansed and healed by Jesus, they can then receive love and grow in the confidence of that love.

Recently I spoke to a mother whose child couldn't bear to be prayed over. Further questioning revealed that part of his inheritance was in witchcraft. After praying and breaking that curse, he was quite happy to have his mother pray.

Another case was that of a nine year old girl with inherited rejection who was always defying her mother, and was easily hurt and often angry. Her mother, who had other children, knew she needed help and feared how her daughter's defiant attitude would manifest when she became a teen-ager. I prayed with her parents as she played outside. As we finished the girl unexpectedly ran inside with a bunch of flowers for her mother, and has been a different child ever since—much happier, not easily hurt, and much softer. How much better to pray when a child is young instead of waiting to see if the child will grow out of the difficult behavior.

Mothers especially know the difference between when their children are normally naughty, and when there is a problem—it's frustrating to be told the behavior is normal when we know it's not. Problems that are small when our children are small get bigger as our children get bigger. Little sins become big sins. Bad behavior and rebellion have bigger consequences. Jesus gives us the tools—we need to learn how to use them.

God's desire is for his people to be holy and set apart, and that includes our children. But so often we don't understand what it is that is holding us back, and what to do about it. We need to ask for wisdom, so as not to be a "people destroyed from lack of knowledge" (Hosea 4:6), and we need to be prepared, like David, to ask God to search our hearts and see if there is any wicked thing there,[5] as our hearts are so deceitful that we don't always see our own sin. It is God's understanding we need—not ours.

The need to be free of sin and its influences on our lives is vital for us, and just as vital for our children. We need to give them a free inheritance so that they have a strong foundation on which to build their lives.

In the case of older children who have not had prayer for their inherited sin, and have consequently sinned in that area themselves, they need not only prayer for the sinful inheritance, but also they need to repent of their personal sin in that area. As soon as children are old enough to be responsible for their own sin, they need to be brought to repentance and helped to understand that they are responsible before God for that sin. They also need to be assured of the Lord's immediate and amazing forgiveness, so that they are not further burdened with guilt and condemnation, which is not of God. Assure your children that God not only sends His Holy Spirit to convict us of our sin, but that He is swift and faithful to forgive us, and, in fact, to *forget* our sin (Jeremiah 31:34 and Hebrews 10:17). If we're feeling guilty and condemned, it's not from God. He convicts us with compassion, love, and firmness.

As I shared the thoughts of this chapter with one of my prayer partners just recently, she told of her continual battle with fear, and came to the realization that she had not only inherited it from her mother, but that other members of the family in the next generation were also affected by it. We prayed for her and she was immediately released. More good news is that once we are free in a particular area, we can pray for others of our family for their freedom, which is what this woman did.

Recently a young woman called to encourage me and to tell me of the wonderful answers she was experiencing from a prayer time I had with her. Among other things, she had been released from a hereditary spirit of fear, and, consequently, recognized the same spirit in her son. I encouraged her to pray for her son herself, in much the same way I had prayed with Cam about his fear. It's important to come to God ourselves in situations such as this, instead of always feeling that we need someone else to help—although there's nothing wrong with asking for help. God always honors us when we sincerely want to learn and grow, and when we pray with our children He will encourage and strengthen our faith much more than if someone else does it for us.

Below is a prayer by Phyl Gibson. It's one that has been extremely helpful and powerful in the lives of our children and of other children. Praying this prayer is a declaration to Satan and the powers of darkness that your child is also a child of the living God. When God spoke it was powerful (Genesis 1:3, 6, 9, 14, 20, 24, 28, 29). When we speak in the name of His Son, our Lord Jesus Christ, it is also powerful. So I encourage you to tell the enemy where you and your household stand. Say with Joshua, "as for me and my household, we will serve the Lord" (Joshua 24:15).

Now this isn't a *quick-fix,, once only*, type prayer, but rather a *clearing the decks because now we know where we stand* type prayer. We cannot assume that our children will automatically become followers of Jesus just because we are. There is much more to be done and much to learn, but it's exciting—be encouraged! "I am the Lord, the God of all mankind. Is anything too hard for me?" (Jeremiah 32:27).

Phyl Gibson's Prayer for Children:

I take authority over you, Satan, and speak to you in the Name of Jesus Christ, and render you powerless in the life of (name of child).

I bind and break your power and loose (child's name) from your control.

All dominations of heredity (name each one—e.g. freemasonry, occult involvement, fear, lust, anger, rejection). I bind and break in the Name of Jesus (name and break every bad habit).

I cleanse the conscious mind, subconscious mind, imagination, emotions, heart, and will by the blood of Jesus Christ.

Lord, keep (name)'s heart open and tender to
the Holy Spirit. I claim (name)'s soul for you, Jesus.
Fill (name) now with your healing, your love,
your peace, and your joy.
I ask this for your glory, and in the name of Jesus.
Amen.[6]

This prayer is particularly appropriate to pray over
a young child or baby who is asleep, especially in the
area of generational sin. The prayer also contains
wonderful tools of wisdom to be used in prayer.
"Cleansing of the conscious mind, subconscious mind,
imagination, emotions, heart and will by the blood of
Jesus Christ" is so important, and I've prayed that
regularly—often daily—for our children. When you see
what they are subjected to on television alone, even the
news, they will need this prayer. Teachers can
occasionally be pushed to the limit of their patience, as
we can also, and come out with negative words—like
stupid, annoying, useless, ignorant, dumb—that can take
hold in a child's mind. Praying regularly for cleansing
will allow the Lord to heal on the spot, and not allow that
crack of legal entry for Satan.

Praying for that "tender and open heart" for the Holy
Spirit is a bit like keeping the ground plowed and ready for
the sowing of the seed. "Claiming their soul for Jesus" is
like taking possession of the seed, and "fill him with your
love, your peace and your joy" is like sowing the seed.

Be encouraged to use prayers such as this often so
that they become a natural part of your daily prayer for
your children. Be encouraged also to ask the Holy Spirit
to teach you how to pray for your children, because it

was from this request that Phyl Gibson was given this special prayer.

Inherited sin can be a difficult concept to explain to a child. As I have suggested, it's often more appropriate to pray for a small child either when they're asleep or absent—and this would be a much more appropriate way to pray through inherited sins in the sexual area. However, the more our children understand the things of God and participate in prayer, the quicker they will mature and "own their own faith."

Often I've used the example of inherited physical features to explain to children what inherited sin means. For example, you might say to a child, "in the same way that you've inherited your father's beautiful blue eyes, you've inherited my fear. We don't need to do anything about the blue eyes because that's the way God made you, but we can do something about the fear, because that's not something that God wants us to have. It's a sin to have unnatural fears, so we need to tell Jesus we're sorry, and ask Him to take it from us."

You might realize that you've inherited a negative emotion from your parents, and you might not have dealt with it yourself, in which case both you and your child can pray about it together. As you come to God in faith and humility, your child will grow in trust and faith—you both will. Your child will respect you for your confession of sin, will learn from it, and will see you in a relationship of faith and trust towards God.

You can even suggest to your children that they use their imaginary swords of the Spirit and with a couple of good swishes and swipes, ask God to set them free from the sin. It's really helpful if you can find a Scripture verse to back up what's been done and learn it together. In the

26

example of fear you could use, "Perfect love drives out fear" (1 John 4:18), or, "God did not give us a spirit of fear, but of power, and of love and of a sound mind" (2 Timothy 1:7).

You could also make up a tune to it and sing it together—you'll be achieving lots of things if you do this. You'll be declaring to the enemy together that you have the victory in Jesus, you'll be having fun, you'll be building up your faith, you'll be making your relationship stronger by sharing something very special, and you'll be teaching your child about spiritual warfare and prayer. You could also find together some good examples in the Bible of people overcoming fear by faith—such as Gideon, Joshua, Daniel in the lions' den, David when he fought Goliath, and read them together. But make it fun and not a chore, and then you'll both enjoy the victory you'll have.

Another helpful method of follow up is to speak positive, affirming, thoughts into your children while they're asleep. If, for example, you've prayed for the breaking of hereditary sins in the area of rejection, I would encourage you to tell your children while they're asleep that they are much loved, by you and by God. If the prayer has been in the area of fear, you could speak courage into the child's spirit and maybe a passage of Scripture. For example, "Do not fear, for I am with you; do not be dismayed, for I am your God. I will strengthen you and help you; I will uphold you with my righteous right hand" (Isaiah 41:10). You'll be pleasantly surprised how children change with this sort of prayer soaking into their spirits.

3

Pray For Your Children

I pray for them. I am not praying for the world, but for those you have given me, for they are yours. All I have is yours, and all you have is mine.

(John 17:9-10)

I have made you known to them, and will continue to make you known in order that the love you have for me may be in them and that I myself may be in them.

(John 17:26)

Those are the words of Jesus to His Heavenly Father shortly before His arrest, concerning first His disciples and then all believers. They can well apply to us as parents when we contemplate how to pray effectively for our children, especially if we consider them to be our primary disciples. And just as Jesus showed forth to His disciples the love of His Father and prayed for them, so we need to be, in the way we live our lives, a demonstration to our children of Jesus' love and life. Jesus was transparent

29

to His disciples—He lived with them, ate with them, slept with them, talked with them, and walked with them.

Jesus taught His disciples and sent them out to do what He was doing. He prayed for them and constantly taught them about His relationship with His Father— in effect, He introduced them to His Father. We parents don't just need to teach our children about Jesus, we need to inspire them to live like Jesus. What a challenging model He has given us if we apply the same principles to discipling of our children. The Israelite parents were told to, "Teach them [the commandments] to your children, talking about them when you sit at home and when you walk along the road, when you lie down and when you get up" (Deuteronomy 11:19).

In other words, not just when maybe we pray before going to bed, or read Bible stories, or when we go to church or Sunday School, but teaching a constant and ever-present relationship with Jesus, so that your children know the truth of Jesus' words to His disciples when He sent them out with His authority. "All authority in heaven and on earth has been given to me. Therefore go . . . And surely I am with you always, to the very end of the age" (Matthew 28:18, 20).

The primary instinct in a mother for her young is protection. So we need to know how to protect our children. Let's extend this natural instinct to protect our children from the dangers of fire, poisons, electricity, traffic, deep water, etc., to the possibility that their spirits can be hurt or damaged. If we could only see the spirits of our children as we can clearly see their bodies, we might see a startling picture. We're horrified when we see pictures of starving and malnourished children living in poverty. We need to see that an under-nourished and starving spirit is just as much cause for concern. Jesus told us that He himself is food and drink to our spirits.

> *I am the living bread that came down from heaven. If anyone eats of this bread, he will live forever. This bread is my flesh, which I will give for the life of the world.*
>
> (John 6:51)

> *Jesus answered and said to her, "Everyone who drinks of this water will be thirsty again, but whoever drinks of the water I give him shall never thirst. The water I give him shall become in him a spring of water welling up to eternal life."*
>
> (John 4:13, 14)

Introducing your children to Jesus by talking about Him, and talking to Him in prayer, will be that food to their spirits. The Scriptures are food to our spirits. We need to pray that our children will come to recognize the need for this "food," just as they understand the need for food that nourishes their bodies. Loving and affirming your children for themselves—for who they are rather than how they act—and spending your love and energy on them, will cause them to grow strong, and give them that physical demonstration of the love of God the Father in their lives.

These two obvious needs—protection and food—in the spiritual dimension of our children's lives need to start at conception. Our children need protection and food in the womb in a physical sense, so why not spiritually?

Jesus said, "Holy Father, protect them by the power of your name" (John 17:11). From the moment of conception, we need to be aware that our child needs prayer for protection.

Dr. Thomas Verny, in his book, *The Secret Life of the Unborn Child,* comes to some important conclusions::

> The fetus can see, hear, experience, taste, and on a primitive level, even learn in the uterus. Most importantly, he can feel, not with an adult's sophistication, but feel nevertheless. ... A corollary to this discovery is that what a child feels and perceives begins shaping his attitudes and expectations about himself. Whether he ultimately sees himself and, hence, acts as a happy or sad, aggressive or meek, secure or anxiety-ridden person, depends, in part, on messages he gets about himself in the womb. The chief source of these shaping messages is the child's mother. This does not mean that every fleeting worry, doubt, or anxiety a woman has rebounds on her child. Chronic anxiety or a wrenching ambivalence about motherhood can leave a deep scar on the unborn child's personality. On the other hand, such life-enhancing emotions as joy, elation and anticipation can contribute significantly to the emotional development of a healthy child.[7]

It then follows that a child who is much anticipated with love, is familiar with his or her mother's and father's voices singing and speaking, and whose mother is free of excessive worry, fear, and sickness during her pregnancy, will have a strong and good foundation on which to build. Dr. Verny gives numerous examples in his book of the effect of prenatal experiences on children, both negative and positive. Obviously, it is not always possible, although desirable, to have a pregnancy free of fear or illness or bad experiences. The wonderful news is that as Christians we have access to healing in Jesus for negative experiences or influences our children may have experienced in the womb.

The birth of a child can be a traumatic time for both mother and baby, and, if this is so, there needs to be much prayer if it is not to have negative effects on the child's life. When I first heard of this concept, I was hesitant to jump in and pray about the reasonably difficult birth of our daughter, Maggie. I had learned that inducing labor often causes the child to have an apprehensive or hesitant spirit, and an insecure approach to life in general. This certainly applied to Maggie, and I had often wondered and worried about it. This whole situation became a most wonderful lesson to me.

First I asked God to show me if there was a need for prayer, and I asked Him for wisdom as to how to approach it. Nothing happened for a couple of months. Then one day when Maggie was about eight years old, she stayed home from school because she been ill during the night. During the day I felt the prompting of the Holy Spirit telling me, "now is the time to pray with her about her birth." Cautiously, I told her that after her birth, I had been rather consumed with my own reactions—anger and disappointment at not being able to accomplish an easy birth, and my exhaustion after a long and difficult labor. I told her that I wanted to apologize to her for being too consumed with my own emotions and not realizing that she would have experienced emotions too. She readily forgave me, and we prayed and I asked the Lord to forgive me.

At that point, Maggie hesitantly told me that she was seeing a vision, or a picture in her mind as she called it, which was puzzling her. In the vision, she was in a dark tunnel, with her hands held out trying to "stop myself being pushed forward because I don't want to go!" I was so excited. The Lord had really honored my prayer. He had shown her the exact experience of induced labor without her having any idea what it was.

We prayed through the whole experience, asking the Lord to heal her of the fear and apprehension of going where she didn't feel ready to go. She then told me of another vision. This time she had obviously been born, but was "being handed round to lots of different people, and I don't know who I belong to." This obviously referred to the fact that she had been in the birth canal a little too long and was a bit blue, so she was put in a humidicrib (incubator) as soon as possible after birth, and many nurses tended to her. Our lack of bonding and close relationship as she grew up had no doubt stemmed from the emotions she felt at that time.

We prayed again for forgiveness—ignorance is not justification in God's sight—and asked the Lord to heal and restore, and to bond us together as we should have been at her birth. Obviously, the Lord delights to do this! Jesus came to bind up the broken hearted and surely He did this for us. Immediately there was a change in our relationship. It was wonderful, and slowly over a couple of months, we saw our daughter change from a hesitant, withdrawn, and slightly over-serious little girl into a confident and fun-loving child.

This doesn't mean that every child who is born by induced labor will have this experience. In fact, Cam was born that way, although a much easier labor, and I didn't feel it necessary to pray with him about it, though I did ask the Lord to heal him of the experience, and he certainly didn't have the symptoms Maggie had. However, if you desire with all your heart to see your children set free to be the people the Lord planned them to be, ask Him to show you the areas of your or your child's life needing prayer, and He will show you. In addition, the act of forgiving each other is crucial to the Lord being able to heal, not only our bodies but also our relationships.

It surely also follows that more serious and traumatic birth difficulties, such as the cord being wrapped round the baby's neck, surgery before or during birth, the death of a twin, attempted abortion, premature birth, and forceps deliveries are all examples of the need for prayer. I have prayed for people who were not wanted by their parents, or were a disappointment because of their sex, and seen great changes. In my experience, all adopted children need prayer because, in their spirits if not necessarily in their minds, there is a knowing that they are not with their natural mother or father, and there is often deep rejection in these children that reaches well into adulthood.

Children with disabilities are nearly always a disappointment to their parents—at least initially—and these children need much prayer. Now don't go looking for problems, but do pray through these things. They can have deep rooted effects on our children, and we need to be clear on one thing—Satan is no respecter of little babies and children. He will enter, influence, distort, destroy, and torment wherever he has legal access to do so.

A word of caution. There are various New Age techniques being used by New Age practitioners where a process called "rebirthing" occurs that may sound similar to what was described with our daughter. With this procedure, one can supposedly relive the birth experience and other babyhood, childhood, and past experiences, and in the recall, re-experience the emotion and in some way learn to overcome it. This procedure is not necessary for a Christian, and it can even be harmful. If the Holy Spirit is in control, the emphasis will be on repentance and it won't be necessary to relive each experience, but rather to deal with the root of the sinful attitude that developed from the experience—such as anger, fear, rejection, bitterness.

Another great need for our children is discernment. Children are born with more spiritual discernment than we realize, and gradually, usually with our encouragement, they are taught not to rely on it, but rather to discern things solely by reason and intellect. Now reason and intellect are not undesirable things, they are indeed gifts from God, but we need to balance them with spiritual discernment. From television, our children receive such a barrage of violence, sex, and conflicting moral values, that they are going to need every bit of discernment possible to help them find a path through.

I've been most encouraged with answers to prayer in this area. In fact I've seen amazing discernment in quite young children of four and five years. Ask the Father to give your children discernment, a real desire and love for the things of God, and a horror and revulsion of the things of the enemy. Then encourage and help them sharpen their discernment by asking them what their reaction is to certain things on television or in books— you'll find they will begin to censure things themselves. That doesn't mean you never need to impose censorship yourself. There will be times when you need to be firm about what you want them to see or read. But talk and pray over it with your children, consider what they believe they're discerning, and treat their opinions with respect, while always bearing in mind that you're in authority and sometimes you need to exercise that authority.

Children are much more discerning about the emotional environment in which they live than we give them credit for. If there is tension and difficulty in their parents' marriage, young children will be aware of it in their spirits. They may not understand exactly what it is that is worrying them from an intellectual point of view, but it will make them feel unsettled and unhappy, and will possibly result in disruptive and difficult behavior. One of the most effective ways of ensuring our children are peaceful is to make sure all is right in our marriage. Peace and love in a marriage is the most stabilizing atmosphere we can provide for our children, and a precious gift to them—more so than material possessions and social opportunities.

Children are often concerned if their parents are ill or unduly worried about something. Again, they may not understand, but they react in their spirits. A friend of mine recently looked after her three-year old grandson. During that time, she had a bad cold and hardly any voice, and it was necessary that she temporarily leave him with someone else. He was most unsettled and unhappy about it, when normally he would have been content. Prompted by the Holy Spirit, she explained to him why her voice sounded strange, and assured him that she would be back to normal in a day or two. He immediately quieted down and went off quite happily without her.

If this child had been older, an explanation would not have been necessary because he would have known in his mind from past experience that his grandmother would get better. This child's spirit was picking up the distress, and it was to the child's spirit she needed to give reassurance. Once that assurance was given, he had peace. Please understand, our children's spirits are more mature than their minds, and spiritually we need to treat them more like adults in little bodies—with intellects that are not yet as developed as adults.

Our son Duncan is a good example of this. He is still unable to speak, but because his spirit is healed and mature, he picks up things in his spirit that he doesn't know how to deal with and cannot express. Recently, we prayed for a young man who had strong hereditary spirits of witchcraft, and who was experiencing great difficulty in other areas of his life. Duncan met him when he arrived for prayer, and was plagued with a bad headache for several days afterwards. We still have much to learn in this area, but after we prayed for Duncan against the effects of the spirits operating in this man's life, his headache stopped. Duncan is in some ways like quite small children. He is highly receptive in his spirit—in fact, he is like a spiritual magnet—but he lacks the discernment and understanding to know what to do with the information he receives in his spirit.

It's important to treat our children with respect—not to humor them or belittle their opinions, their enthusiasms, or their fears. When Cam was quite young, he woke one night screaming and very frightened, and said he had seen a skull and crossbones on his bedroom window blind. He declared he would never sleep in his room again. All sorts of possible reactions went through my mind—how would I handle this one? Should I tell him he was just dreaming, or imagining it all, drag him back into his room with the light switched on and say,

"See, there's nothing here." Instead of any of those, I decided to treat him with respect, believe him, and pray with him.

We spoke to whatever it was in his room and told it to go in the name of Jesus. We asked the Holy Spirit to come and fill every part of his room with His light. We made an imaginary sign of the Cross on his blind, and we asked the Lord to take away the fear and cleanse Cam's mind, subconscious mind, and his imagination. He straight away declared, "It feels much better now," and went back to bed, and back to asleep.

You can pray into every area of your children's lives—it's exciting, and certainly better than worrying. You'll find too that you will get less anxious about them because God will give you the gift of faith in greater measure as you pray. You will also be less possessive of your children, and be able to release them into the Lord's care. He is much more effective and efficient at caring for our children than we are—after all, they're *His* children really.

You can pray about your children's schooling, friends, teachers, subjects, careers, future partners. The list is endless. Sometimes we even get more than we ask or think. I prayed for years for our daughter Maggie's husband, and never thought of asking that he be sensitive to the needs of disabled people—which is what a brother-in-law to Duncan would have to be. The Lord on His own gave Maggie a husband who loves disabled people and has worked with them. God is amazing!

Pray often for your children in the areas of sex, dating, and marriage. In a world that is increasingly saturated with sex, young Christians are walking a minefield. Pray that by the time they reach puberty, they will know how to deal with rejection and rebellion in their lives. Without healing in these areas, they will be easy prey for the enemy in sexual areas. Talk to them about what the Bible has to say on premarital sex. Explain to them that to have sex with someone is to be bonded to them in spirit and they become "one flesh" (Genesis 2.24; 1 Corinthians 6:16). Spirits can and do pass from one person to another when this spiritual bonding occurs in intercourse—it's a bit like "spiritual AIDS." When I explained this to one young man, he said, "I'm so glad you told me that. Now I understand why it's so important." Pray that the Lord will not allow them to be sexually wakened until they meet the partner He has for them, and encourage them when they're old enough to pray it for themselves. In the culture we live in, they make the choice of whom they will marry, but your prayers beforehand will make all the difference.

A powerful way to pray for children is to pray using the Scriptures. We're told in Hebrews 4:12 that "the word of God is living and active . . . sharper than any double-edged sword." Take Scripture verses like Paul's prayer for the Ephesians in Chapter 3:14-21 and personalize them for yourself and your children. When you come across passages in the Scriptures that you would like to apply to your children, personalize them something like this:

> [Original] *I will instruct you and teach you in the way you should go; I will counsel you and watch over you.*
>
> (Psalm 32:8)

[Personalized] Thank you Father that you will instruct my children, (names), and teach them in the way they should go. Thank you that you will counsel and watch over them.

Once you've become familiar with doing that, you'll find it easy to expand the Scriptures even further into specifics for the individual child you're praying for:

Father, I pray that (child's name), will have a real hunger to read your Word so that your Holy Spirit will prompt him and teach him , especially as he struggles with how to know what You would have him do in a particular relationship, or in deciding what subjects to do at school, or understanding the need for repentance or forgiveness in a specific situation.

Thank you, Father, that he is Your child, that You have plans for his life, and that You watch over this child that we share together.

You can also put your children to bed with a praise tape, or read some Scriptures to them, even a single verse will help. Then their spirits can dwell on it while they sleep. I formed a habit of asking the Holy Spirit to cleanse our children every evening, and of sending them off each day with a blessing and prayer for protection, and asking that they be a blessing to everyone they contact. Duncan will not leave for work in the morning without his blessing. Even if society calls him "intellectually disabled," he is not spiritually disabled, and he is indeed a blessing to many people.

Instant Prayers

Another area of prayer for children is what I call "instant prayers." We can't possibly protect our children from hurt, whether it be physical or emotional, all the time. Nor do our prayers have the power to render them totally safe—although I often wonder what unseen dangers they are protected from every day and never know about! Nor would it be wise if we could protect our children from all harm to do so, since it is in suffering and difficult situations that we grow into maturity, and learn to rely on the Lord for all our needs.

"Instant prayers" for little children are particularly helpful in preventing emotional or physical hurts from taking hold of a child and leaving lasting damage. An example of an emotional hurt might be the first encounter with a barking dog—they can look enormous and threatening to a small child. You might need to pray against fear as well as introduce them to a smaller and friendlier dog. A sudden stay in the hospital in a emergency situation is another example where you would need to pray against rejection, abandonment, fear, confusion—also for God's protection, comfort, and security—as well as giving lots of your own. These things can be dealt with on the spot by the Lord if you pray, but if left could easily result in major problems for the child in later life.

Pray Without Ceasing

In summary, PRAY! Paul tells us to pray without ceasing and to pray continually. The Bible tells us that we are at war, that we have an enemy, Satan, who is constantly ready to attack and to claim ground. He is no respecter of babies or children of any age. Don't allow them to start or live their lives in a vulnerable state, unprotected from the unseen spiritual forces that control so much of our world. Jesus has overcome the enemy, and we need to claim His victory for our children. There is no formula by which we can give them a trouble-free life. Jesus told us that we would have trouble in this world, but He overcame the world for us (John 16:33), and as we pray for our children to have the peace that He promised, they will become strong and courageous, and in turn become overcomers themselves.

Trusting God

As we grow in the area of praying for our children, we'll grow in faith and develop a greater trust in God regarding our children. We then become much more positive in our attitudes towards dangers they face. At the moment I write this, Cam has just left for the beach to surf. Before learning to trust the Lord, I would have been inclined to farewell him with words something like: "Be careful and watch out for sharks, blue bottles, other surfers, and big waves." If I didn't say something like that, I would think about all the dangers he faced and worry about him until he came home.

But because I've learned more about prayer, spiritual warfare, and faith , I've just farewelled him with: "Take care and have a good surf." Then I said to the Lord, "Thank you Lord that he's in your hands. Please direct your angels to protect him and thank you that "even the winds and the waves obey you" (Matthew 8:27).

Cam has also learned to pray for himself. When farewelling on a surfing holiday recently, he casually said to me, "Don't worry, Mum, we always pray before we surf, especially the big ones."

Songs of Safety

Little children need to be aware of dangers they face, both physical and spiritual, but we need to be thoughtful and not express fear by what we say. Instead of "if you're not careful crossing the street, you'll get run over," which is a fearful and negative thing to say, try teaching them a song like the one often heard on ABC Playschool—the chorus goes like this:

> Well we stop!
> (Yes, we stop.)
> And we look!
> (Yes, we look.)
> And we listen.
> Nothing coming?
> Then we go.[8]

Learn the whole song and sing this with appropriate actions every time you cross the road with them—make it a fun game. Then, when they're old enough to go on their own, leave them in God's hands and thank Him—and if you think they'll forget the song, ask the Holy Spirit to remind them.

Angels

Talk to your children about angels and how they can protect us in emergency situations, and teach them to call on the name of Jesus if they find themselves in an emergency. If children hear you talking to Jesus in everyday situations where you need help—asking for a parking space, remembering someone's name, or asking forgiveness for being irritable or judgmental, it will become second nature to them as well as to you. You'll both grow in faith and victory, and God will demonstrate His love for you in many ways. Maggie came home from a field hockey match one day and told how she had been pulled quite strongly by an unseen force from the path of a ball that would have hit her in the head. "He will command his angels concerning you to guard you in all your ways" (Psalm 91:11)—and that includes our children.

Plain Talk in Prayer

Language is most important in praying with children. There is some wonderful language used in the Bible, especially in the Psalms and the Books of the Prophets. The imagery is wonderful and will be appreciated as your children grow older, but it's important, also, to teach them that prayer is simply talking with God. Try to use the language you would use when talking about anything else, and avoid religious words that they may not understand, especially when you pray. For example, instead of using words such as sin, confession, and repentance, which little children won't understand, we can talk about things that are wrong, things that make God disappointed with us or sad. Instead of confession, we can talk about telling Jesus we're sorry, and repentance is being sorry enough not to do it again. You might find substituting these words difficult, but it's important and fits in well with the concept that God

45

can be included in every facet of life. It can also be a challenge to us because as we simplify concepts and get away from religious words, we often find we understand the concept and words much clearer ourselves.

Teenagers also need to be encouraged to talk to the Lord in their everyday language. Even if you don't understand all the words and in-phrases they use, God does. It will make their relationship with Him so much more real if they feel free to talk to Him in the language they use for their friends, instead of the language of the official prayer book of your church, or the language of your particular version of the Bible.

Hearing from God

Prayer is also hearing from God, and children will hear Him easily if you encourage them in this. Teach them that they don't have to be praying to hear from God. We can all hear from God at anytime, wherever we are, and whatever we're doing. If you hear something from God, share it with them if you can, and ask them if they believe it lines up with the Scriptures, and how they feel about it in their spirits. When you do this, you'll find that they will then share with you the things they feel God is telling them. You might even get your Bibles and check the Scriptures—this is much more natural, fun, and challenging than always having a formal Bible study—though there's nothing wrong with a formal Bible study. It's just that an informal one is more fun for most children.

Relationship With God

Your children should see your relationship with Jesus and the Scriptures as absolutely necessary and precious to

46

you, and also enriching, fun, exciting, and real. When they see this in your life, they will want to know this wonderful God for themselves. It's not unlike having a wonderful friend whom you talk to your children about. If you make that friend sound special, exciting, wise, and fun, they will eventually ask you, "When can I meet this super friend of yours?"

As you nurture this wonderful relationship of yours with God, and encourage your children in it as well, you'll find your relationship with your children will deepen and flourish. You'll also find that the intermingling of your relationship with God and your children will have a spiritual effect upon others. Cam and a boy named Dan have been special friends since they were five. After watching Cam and me during many trips home in the car from football practice, Dan asked if he could come to church with us. He later gave his life to Jesus, and so did his mother and sister. We didn't preach to Dan, we just sometimes talked about Jesus during our everyday conversation as we "walked along the road" (Deuteronomy 11:19). If you talk about someone you love with great enthusiasm, most people will want to know that person also.

4

Teach Your Children to Pray

One day Jesus was praying in a certain place. When he finished, one of his disciples said to him, "Lord, teach us to pray, just as John taught his disciples."

He said to them, "When you pray, say: "'Father, hallowed be your name, your kingdom come.

Give us each day our daily bread.

Forgive us our sins, for we also forgive everyone who sins against us. And lead us not into temptation.'"

(Luke 11:1-4)

The greatest things we can teach our children is how to know the Lord, and how to talk to Him in prayer. In doing this, we should not try too hard, nor insist on rigid regularity in praying, but rather show our children that praying should spring naturally from a relationship that is deeply satisfying and fulfilling. Our own prayer life should be something our children want for themselves, rather than something we tell them they ought to have. In the foreword to Dr. Ross Campbell's book, *How to Really Know Your Child,* Andy Butcher writes, "I've met many Christian parents whose admirable and burning desire for their children is to come to faith in Jesus. This has been the very thing—suffocating in its intensity and rigidity—that has made that increasingly unlikely as the years go by."[9]

When we look at Jesus and the way He prayed, we see no rigidity or suffocation, no formulas or methods for a successful prayer life. We see Jesus in constant communication with His heavenly Father, desiring that communication, going off alone and seeking His Father's presence, and then being so close to His Father that He only did what His Father told Him to do. Isn't that prayer? His ministry flowed out of His relationship with His Father. That's what we should desire for our children as we minister to them.

God the Father and Heaven

One of the first things our children need to know in order to pray properly is what their Father in heaven is like. Most children unconsciously base their perception of God the Father on the characteristics of their earthly father. Children who have had an overly authoritarian father will see God chiefly as a stern figure of authority. Those who have had a frequently absent father will see God as one who is not interested in small, everyday, concerns. Those who have had little discipline and have been spoiled by their fathers will see God as an over indulgent figure ready to overlook their sins. So the more that earthly fathers model their lives on Jesus, the healthier their children's perception of their heavenly Father will be. It needs to be said early and often to children that earthly Dads and Moms, although they love their children dearly, cannot possibly always be there for them, but their heavenly Father can. Earthly parents can and do make mistakes. Their heavenly Father does not. Earthly parents can't always be relied upon. Their heavenly Father can. He will be with them always, to the end of the age (Matthew 28:20), and that's the basis for that transference of dependence from us, as parents, to God—which is the ultimate of "owning one's own faith." Children have wonderfully imaginative ideas about the whole area of heaven, and we should never discourage them in their thoughts about it. Instead, we should emphasize the promises of God—no more sadness or crying or pain, only great peace and joy, and living with Jesus forever.

Children's concepts of heaven can be a great delight, and may be closer to the truth than some of our concepts.. Only God knows. Cam had an early concept of God in heaven with a huge computer on which He pressed buttons and caused things to happen on earth. I still recall with pleasure seven-year old Maggie's remarks when learning of her grandmother's death on Christmas Day: "Isn't it wonderful? She'll be there in time for the Birthday Party!" She obviously had a marvelous picture of this huge birthday party for Jesus on Christmas Day, with her grandmother in attendance, and free from the pain and suffering she endured before her death. What a comforting thought it was for us to hold to as we struggled with her loss.

Maybe the most important thing we can get across to our children is God's enormous and constant love for them. Most children seem to need a continual reassuring that God really does want to lavish His love on them. We should also tell them that however wonderful they imagine heaven is going to, it is going to be far better than that. God has promised us, and the Apostle Paul has told us, "No eye has seen, no ear has heard, no mind has conceived what God has prepared for those who love him" (1 Corinthians 2:9).

One day when Cam was quite small, still not old enough to read, he asked what I thought heaven is like. I called on God for wisdom and said something like this:

> See how I can read all the words in this newspaper and you can't yet? Well, that's because your brain isn't grown up enough to read a newspaper. It will be one day. It's the same about Heaven. We haven't grown up enough to understand exactly what Heaven's like. We probably won't understand properly until we get to Heaven. I think maybe God wants it to be a wonderful surprise for us.

The answer seemed to satisfy him, and it was in words and concepts he understood.

Praying About Animals

When our children were small we got a kitten for them, but the dog we had did not exactly welcome her with open paws. There were wild scenes of chasing, snarling, and bristling hair standing on end. After a few days, Maggie said to me, "Mum, you know that bit in the Bible about the wolf lying down with the lamb? Could we pray that for Lassie and Fudge?" So we did, with amazing results! They almost immediately drank out of the same bowl, curled up and went to sleep together, and were great friends until Lassie died. We've continued to pray that prayer over all our animals ever since.

Praise and Worship

Little children will respond quickly to praise and worship because of their spiritual awareness, but they may need help to get started in learning how to express themselves. We should teach them early in their lives that church and Sunday school are not the only places to worship God, and that they should praise and worship God everyday *for* everything and *in* everything. Here are some examples we might use to help them learn.

"Doesn't this grass feel wonderful under your feet? Thank you, Jesus, for making it."

"Isn't it amazing how every one of these flowers is different? See how beautiful they are. Isn't God wonderful to make them all so special?"

"God is so thoughtful the way He made your pet just so you could take such special care of him—thanks God!"

"Isn't snow incredible the way it feels so cold and crunchy? God must have the most amazing imagination—thanks heaps God."

"It's just as well God made my finger hurt right away when I burned it—otherwise I might have left it where it was and burned it really badly— God's so clever!"

"Aren't you glad God made us so we can feel good when we hug each other, and forgive each other?"

When you and your children come across an exhilarating sight—mountains, oceans, sunsets, beautiful clouds, be exhilarated! Yell, scream, dance, or sing your pleasure and praise! Once while walking along a deserted beach early one Easter Sunday morning and feeling the exultation and sense of victory of Jesus rising from the dead, I found a stick and wrote in big letters JESUS IS ALIVE along the beach—then I shouted it out loud as a spirit of praise and joy flowed through me; even the very waves seemed to join in! If you can inspire your children to have a passion for Jesus, then most assuredly He'll reveal Himself to them in deeper intimacy.

Some of the old hymns make marvelous marching music when you're out walking and little ones are getting a bit weary. Try a rendition of marching and acting out bits of *Onward Christian Soldiers* and see how the atmosphere can change.

There's so much wonderful contemporary praise music available for you and your children. Play it often and sing it yourself. Encourage your children to make up their own—there's a wealth of words in the Psalms that they can use. Teach them that praise is not only for God but also for them, and that it will make them feel happy. If you can encourage your children to praise God in the spirit, you will be seeing that their spirits are fed. As they praise Him and read the Scriptures, their spirits will be nurtured and grow healthy, just as their bodies will when you make sure they have the right food and exercise.

Thanksgiving

As a child I wondered why it seemed the Christians thing to do to thank God for the necessities of life, when it seemed obvious to me that food was on the table and clothes were in the cupboard because Dad worked and made money, and Mom went out and bought everything. Don't assume that children understand our adult perception of God's provision.

When saying grace, it's a good idea to be original and spontaneous about giving thanks. In our family, my husband usually prays before our meal and we all hold hands. But if he is away, as he often is, the person who sits at the head of the table prays. With little children, meal time is a good opportunity to emphasize the fact that all things come from God. Often we thank Him for every item in our meal, and even the ingredients in the food and where they came from. It's also a good time to thank Him for the work the parents do, and the children's schooling and teachers. The main thing to get across is that God is the source of all our daily necessities, and He should be thanked everyday for them.

Hearing from God

We need to encourage our children not only to speak to God, but also to hear from God. They need to be sure they hear from Him before they can own their own faith, and it's a skill we all need to acquire. As with all skills, the more we practice, the more adept we become. The closer we are to someone, the more we will instinctively know their heart, their attitude, and their mind, and we will trust them—so it is with our children and God. Jesus said, "My sheep hear My voice," and they *will* hear *if* they learn to listen. Just as in the days when Jesus walked this earth and the shepherds had small flocks whose lambs stayed with their mothers until they knew the shepherd's voice, so will our children learn to hear our Shepherd's voice if they're encouraged to practice. We should always check out what they're hearing, however, and make certain it lines up with the Scriptures.

When Cam was five, he announced one morning, "God just told me I don't have to go to school today". This was obviously an occasion that called for discretion and fast prayer! I did want to encourage him to hear from God, but it could become too easy for him to preface his occasional selfish whim with, "God told me," which, as we all know, is not easy to argue with. On this occasion, I told Cam that I had intended to go out that day and thought that was what God wanted me to do, so obviously "one of us had our wires crossed." We agreed that we would both go back to God and check with Him. Somewhat chastened, although not entirely defeated, Cam came back with, "Well, God does want me to have a day off, but it's not today." Much relief all round. He never tried that one again, but he does now hear from God.

Don't be hesitant about encouraging children to hear from God in difficult situations. When Maggie's beloved dog, Lassie, was run over and died in her arms, I thought, "how is the Lord possibly going to comfort her in this?" and, "maybe she'll be mad at God for letting this happen.?" O ye of little faith, the Lord was saying to me! Even though weak in faith, I prayed with Maggie and asked God to comfort her. Naturally, He did! She had a vision of Jesus playing with Lassie, perfectly clean and well, by a perfect stream on perfect grass, fetching sticks out of the water. I don't know about the theological correctness of dogs in Heaven. I only know that our distraught little daughter was immediately comforted and at peace.

Weeks later, she confided in me that Jesus had told her that He had allowed Lassie to die because Maggie had poured everything into her dog, and that Jesus wanted that place in her life. Heavy stuff for a primary school child, but the Lord knows our children better than we do, and knows what they can handle. He also told her she would get another dog, and she did, some years later, but she learned her lesson early and well.

It's wonderful to acquire this hearing skill as children. We should make it a habit to ask our children questions like, "What do you think God wants you to do on this occasion?" Try small decisions first, such as, "Would God want you to watch this TV show?" or "How can I make friends with this person, or "Why is my friend so angry?" That way, by the time the big decisions about such things as careers and marriage have to be made, and major discernment is needed, you can be confident your children will be hearing their Shepherd's voice.

God's Plan for Your Children

Teach your children early that God does have a plan for their lives, but that it's up to them to find out what that plan is and to cooperate with God in fulfilling it. We also need to assure them that God's plan will be much more exciting and rewarding than anything you or they could plan. Assure them, also, that any gifts that God has given them will be part of that plan—show them what the Lord told Jeremiah: "For I know the plans I have for you," declares the Lord, "plans to prosper you and not to harm you, plans to give you hope and a future" (Jeremiah 29:11).

Admittedly these are words directed at his exiled people in Babylon, but they can be readily applied to His children of the New Covenant as they come into their "promised land" of freedom and life in Christ, their New Covenant redeemer and deliverer.

Receiving and Giving

When praying with your children for your daily necessities, ask God to give your family not only enough for its own needs, but also enough over so that you can give to others. If we teach our children that God is generous in giving, and so we should be the same, God will bless them abundantly. As a result they will grow up with an attitude of freely receiving and freely giving, and will be free from greed and hoarding for themselves. Being free, they will know the joy of God giving to them abundantly so that He can use them to give to others who need His help.

I love the story of our pastor who, early in his life, gave away a guitar. He says that ever since then his family has never lacked a guitar—whenever he's needed one, someone has given him one. Again, it's that attitude of freely giving and freely receiving. It's as if God is able to give us more if we don't have an attitude of hanging on to things and keeping them for ourselves.

God's Forgiveness

Forgiveness is one of the factors that separates Christianity from every other religion. No other religion has a God who forgives sins. Not only does God forgive our sins, but He also says, "I will . . . remember their sins no more" (Jeremiah 31:34). (See also Isaiah 43:25.)

It's a wonderfully liberating experience to know that we can be forgiven, no matter what we have done, if we go to God with a repentant heart and a determination to turn from sin. So it's never too early to teach our children to ask God for forgiveness for wrong doing, wrong saying, and wrong feelings. Once they learn that God will forgive them if they ask Him to, we need to teach them that most people will do the same thing if they ask for their forgiveness.

One day when Maggie was about 6 and Cam 4, we had one of those times when they argued and fought all day. In desperation I loaded all three children into the car and took off for a big park with swings and slides in an effort to clear the air before bath time.

Some time after we got there, Cam disappeared. I thought he was probably "playing for attention," but Maggie, because we had sometimes lost Duncan and had to call the police to help find him, became worried about Cam, in spite of her bad relationship with him that day.

My instinct was correct, however, and as we pretended to leave without him, he appeared from behind a big rock, looking quite smug. We then went home for bath and tea. Later, when Maggie was climbing out of her bath, she casually remarked, "I feel so much better now that all my boxes are gone."

I had no idea what she was talking about, and I asked her, "What do you mean, *boxes?*"

She patted her chest and said, "Well, I have Jesus here always, and He makes me feel happy and good. But today, when I started hating Cam, all these heavy boxes came and squashed Jesus, and I couldn't feel Him anymore, and I felt awful. When we lost Cam, I knew I didn't really hate him at all, and now all the boxes are gone and I feel happy again." With that she ran off to her room, satisfied with what to her was an adequate explanation.

As I pondered the wisdom of what she had said, I realized how right it all was. It was obviously the Holy Spirit at work in her. First of all, Maggie had experienced the heaviness that sin brings to our hearts. Second, she knew that Jesus would never leave her, even if it felt as if He had, because she belonged to Him (Hebrews 13:5), and, third, she had let go of her sin and again knew peace. I thought of Jesus' words, "Come to Me, all you who are weary and burdened [with boxes], and I will give you rest" (Matthew 11:28).

Maggie's experience proved to be an effective tool in teaching our children how to unload their sinful attitudes and actions. When their father was away and they were acting up because of it, I would say to them,

"You've got a big box of (fear, anger, jealousy, loneliness, or whatever it was) for Dad. Give it to Jesus and say you're sorry." As they practiced this, it became increasingly easier for them to pray this way and receive instant release. Years later, I had to remind Maggie that it was her prayer from the beginning. We had become so used to praying the "boxes prayer," as we called it, that she had forgotten how it originated. I've even used it myself on occasions, leaning over the kitchen sink when resentment threatened to engulf me because of some incident, and it always brought blissful forgiveness and peace. *God is so good!*

We need to teach our children as early as possible that wrong attitudes are just as sinful as wrong doing and need to be dealt with just as quickly. That way they will learn to cherish the peace that Christ gives them inside themselves, and will shun anything that takes that peace away.

Forgiving Others

Children don't realize that it's not an option to forgive others who sin against them—it's a command. During the Sermon on the Mount, Jesus said, "For if you forgive men when they sin against you, your heavenly Father will also forgive you. But if you do not forgive men their sins, your Father will not forgive your sins" (Matthew 6:14-15).

Fortunately, children are by nature forgiving, so it's not hard to teach them how important it is to forgive others. Hopefully, if they learn this lesson early in life, it will become an automatic response in them to forgive when others hurt them. As they grow in this attitude of forgiveness, it will become a habit that will result in them living free of anger, resentment, bitterness, and other negative emotions. The wonderful thing is that the Lord only requires their will in this, and He will bring their emotions into line with their will afterwards.

Here's an example of that, again from our family. It was Maggie's tenth birthday. There was much excitement, and Cam was somewhat overlooked in all this, and was obviously feeling left out. As a result, he was jealous and very cross, and not at all in the mood to wish his sister a happy birthday.

To try to straighten things out, we went up to his bedroom where we could talk alone about his bad attitude. After much reluctance on his part, and much expressive flinging himself on his bed with accompanying dramatic door slamming, he ungraciously agreed to pray with me about it As we prayed, the Lord reminded Cam about a time when we had given Maggie a horse. Now Cam didn't want a horse, but that incident was the root of the jealousy and resentment that was surfacing at the time of her birthday—it was another time when she was being treated special and he wasn't.

Then, without any suggestion on my part, in his mind Cam saw Jesus at the moment we met Maggie's new horse, but Jesus was admiring the horse and not consoling Cam—which is what I would have imagined would have taken place. Cam told me that the Lord was beckoning him to come to where He was, but that he wasn't going because he was angry at his father and me and jealous of Maggie.

Together we prayed the *boxes prayer,* and Cam laid down his heavy boxes of anger and jealousy. "What's happening now?" I asked.

Cam said, "He's still beckoning me . . . and . . . I'm going!" With that, he jumped from the bed, did a little dance and a whoop, and then proceeded to finish the birthday card he had begrudgingly been making for Maggie. At the bottom of it He wrote, "I hope you have the best Birthday ever! Lots of love and hugs, Cam."

To teach the principles of forgiveness to our children is one of the best gifts we can give them. Once they live with the freedom of forgiveness, they will not want to live with the heaviness and separation from Jesus that unforgiveness brings. They will find freedom much more attractive than heaviness. If negative feelings are left to root in a child, they will become a flourishing garden of negative weeds that will invade and take over the whole person in adulthood.

The Book of Hebrews says, "See to it that no one misses the grace of God and that no bitter root grows up to cause trouble and defile many" (Hebrews 12:15). Forgiveness releases the power of God and brings healing to the soul. In his book, *The House of the Lord*, Francis Frangipane wrote:

It may rend the heavens, as Christ's forgiveness did for us, or it may rend the heart when we forgive one another. Whether the result is spectacular or subtle, however, forgiveness is the very life of God. When Stephen forgave his murderers, a plea for mercy with Saul of Tarsus written on it ascended to the heart of God. Could it have been the divine response to Stephen's forgiveness that was instrumental in transforming Saul into Paul, an apostle of God? [10]

Asking Our Children for Forgiveness

It's important for us as parents to be humble and honest with our children when we need to ask for their forgiveness. Inevitably, we'll unintentionally hurt them, let them down, have misunderstandings, and react badly at times. In these situations, it's vital that we ask their forgiveness. It's not a weakness to appear vulnerable before our children—it's a strength for them and for us. It's a strength for them because it teaches them how to be vulnerable and open with us and, later on, with their close friends. When we ask our children to forgive us for hurting them, we are teaching them to do the same to us and others. It's a strength for us because it enables us to both practice and be humble and honest before those we love the most.

The Apostle Paul wrote, "If you forgive anyone, I also forgive him. And what I have forgiven—if there was anything to forgive—I have forgiven in the sight of Christ for your sake, in order that Satan might not outwit us" (2 Corinthians 2:10-11). " Unforgiveness and bitterness are doorways through which the forces of darkness can enter our lives. Forgiveness opens our hearts to the Holy Spirit who brings freedom, peace, and abundant life. As written in Deuteronomy 30:19, "choose life, so that you and your children may live." We do this by being forgiving Christians, and teaching our children to be the same.

Deliverance from Evil

The whole area of temptation, evil spirits, and the devil can be a complicated one to try and explain to our children, but like anything else, if the basics are understood, the rest will fall into place as time goes on. Just as children have a general spiritual understanding of God, they also grasp very quickly the concept of evil, and often understand it with amazing clarity. When explaining this area, for whatever reason, we should keep it as simple as possible. Perhaps something like this:

Satan was one of God's very special angels that God created before time began. Satan doesn't have a body, like us, so we can't see him, but he's just as real as if he had a body. Satan wasn't happy to be a special angel, the way God made him to be. He wanted to be like God, to have power of his own, and so God sent him away from his special place and quite a few other angels went with him. Satan and his angels or demons work in the opposite way to God. They try to encourage us to do things that we know are wrong, and they want to control us in our thinking, our feelings and the things we do—in fact, they don't want us to believe in God at all, and especially they don't want us to have Jesus in our hearts. But we need to remember that when we have Jesus, we have the power of Jesus, and when Jesus died on the Cross He beat the devil for us. So we can always beat the devil when we use Jesus' name, because we belong to Him. With Jesus on our side we can always win.

Our aim in teaching our children about sin, temptation, the devil and demons is to teach them to be overcomers. To be an overcomer, they need to know their authority and source of power, and to be able to use it, and they need to learn how Satan and his demons will try win them over. Once they've exercised that power and known the victory that Jesus has for them over the powers of evil, they are overcomers and become stronger with each victory. Here's an example from my own experience.

A young friend, Nicolette, started school in her home city when she was five, but after just six months, she and her family moved to another city. Nicolette then had to wait six months before she could attend a new school, and she had to start all over again. Those six months were long and frustrating and she missed her friends. She became very apprehensive and fearful as time went on and she began to imagine how hard it was going to be attending another school with new teachers and no friends. By the time I talked to her about it she had become nervous and fretful.

After talking to her for a while, I encouraged her to confess her fear to Jesus and ask His forgiveness for it, which she did. I explained that Jesus knew all about her family moving interstate—it was probably His idea, and there was no way He wouldn't help her at school if only she would ask Him. I told her that the fear didn't come from God. It came from her mind and her feelings, and that Satan was making it worse because he likes people to be frightened and not trust God, and that's why he had sent a spirit of fear to whisper bad things to her. But she shouldn't believe them because they weren't true.

I then lead her in a simple prayer, something like this. "Thank you Jesus for taking away my fear. Please help me to be strong and to trust you. Thank you that You'll be with me when I go to school. Thank you that you'll choose my teacher and my friends." I then explained to her that the devil would try and get her to be fearful again and this was how she should pray, "Fear, in the name of Jesus, I tell you to go. I am a child of God in Heaven and I don't want you anywhere near me. Perfect love drives out fear, and God did not give me 'a spirit of fear, but of power and of love and of a sound mind'" (1 John 4:18; 2 Timothy 1:7, NKJV).

I was staying with her family at the time, and we prayed this prayer together several times when her problem came up in conversation. When she learned the Scriptures, and gained confidence in the prayer, she started praying it by herself. Just after my visit ended, she went to school. The evening of her first day at school, we talked on the phone and she was joyously triumphant.

Nicolette settled into school very quickly, and was well on the way to being an overcomer. She had learned the principles and applied them herself. She trusted the Lord more at the end of the experience than she had at the beginning. Without question, she'll go on from strength to strength, growing ever stronger—*and she's only five years old!* God rejoices at mighty little overcomers.

Now Nicolette's parents or I could have prayed and assured her that everything was going to be all right, and most likely it would have been. But teaching her to do it herself, with backup, taught her much more and made her much stronger. Eventually, she will own her own faith, just as Cam did his.

Nicolette's little sister, Chantelle, also had a problem with fear, and it was dealt with in a different but equally effective way. She was about three at the time, and was fearful of having nightmares and sleeping in a dark room—not an uncommon fear in children. A pastor suggested to her parents that, as well as praying, they write some Scriptures that promised the Lord's protection and strength in fearful situations and put them on the walls of Chantelle's bedroom. They did this and read them to her. This so encouraged and helped her that she asked for them to be read every night. Before long, she too learned to be a little overcomer. One morning about a year later, she stormed from her room and announced at breakfast, "The devil came into my room last night, but I told him to just GET OUT IN THE NAME OF JESUS, and he did!" No doubt it wasn't the devil himself—nevertheless, the evil spirits that torment will even obey a four-year-old, *if* she knows her authority in Jesus and uses it.

The Courage of Daniel

Get into the habit of using everything that happens, especially the little things, to direct your children toward God and the freedom He brings. If children get used to living in freedom when they're young, they won't want to live with sin and the heaviness it brings as they grow older. For example, when he was six, Cam came home from school one day with some small pieces of chalk. I asked him where he got them from and, in a slightly embarrassed and offhand fashion, he told me that the teacher didn't want them.

On closer questioning, however, he admitted that he assumed that the teacher didn't want them because they were broken. On even closer questioning, he admitted that he took them without permission—in other words, he stole them. He was undoubtedly right, of course. The teacher probably would never miss them and probably didn't want them, but the point of honesty needed to be made—before bigger opportunities came his way.

I told Cam that he would have to take the chalk back. He was quite alarmed at facing the teacher and confessing his deed. So we sat down with the Bible and read the story of Daniel in the lions' den. Cam confessed that he took the chalk without permission, and asked the Lord to forgive him. Then we prayed that he would have the "courage of Daniel."

The next day, Cam came home from school and triumphantly declared, "I got the courage of Daniel and I told the teacher, and she was so nice to me, and asked me to stay after school and help her. I had the best time!"

Can you see all the victories flowing from this one small, seemingly unimportant, incident? First, there's conviction of sin when it would have been easy to disregard it because it was so insignificant; then there was confession and asking God for forgiveness, and then taking the Scriptures about Daniel and making them relevant to the situation.

Having so armed himself, Cam was able to confess and ask forgiveness of the teacher who reacted so well to his honesty and repentance that the incident served to build up his relationship with her. He came away free, light, and happy, instead of being allowed to file away a tiny bit of heaviness and darkness in his spirit where it would have festered and smoldered, waiting for the next opportunity to attract him to sin again in the same area. If these little sins are allowed to build up in our children's lives, they will become unresponsive to the things of the Spirit, and they won't hear the prompting and warnings that the Holy Spirit will be giving them, especially when the big issues confront them as they get older.

Spiritual Warfare

Our children will be tempted, and we need to teach them how to arm themselves for the battle. We are told that "Jesus was led by the Spirit into the desert to be tempted by the devil" (Matthew 4:1).

Francis Frangipane wrote:

> Christians need to accept that the Father is not squeamish about testing his sons and daughters. The word *tempted* in this text means *proven or tested through adversity.* God led Jesus to be tempted in spiritual warfare with the devil himself. ... Luke's Gospel states that Jesus was full of the Holy Spirit during the test. This was not a matter of His flesh falling into temptation, but His character being proven in temptation. Christ was tempted as we are, in His mind, with weakness washing over His soul. To perfect character, the temptations we experience must be real temptations which lead us to real choices. The doubts must have legitimate questions; the fleshly temptations must have credible pleasures. Yet in the face of what Satan hurls, we must remain loyal to God.[11]

As we see our children win the victory in various areas of their lives, we need to encourage them and pray that they will have a stronghold of Christ-likeness built up in their lives. This will have the effect of ensuring they have the mind of Jesus, the love of Jesus, the compassion of Jesus, the wisdom of Jesus, and the power of Jesus.

As our children grow older, we'll see them struggle

with bigger and more dangerous temptations, and it will be in these struggles that we'll see them come forth as overcomers—*if* their foundations are in the rock of Jesus, and *if* they've learned to overcome in the little temptations first, like Nicolette, Chantelle, and Cam. Keep turning your children's eyes back to Jesus, keep encouraging them to live in the Word so that they can call it forth to defeat the enemy, and keep praying for them to be strengthened. Pray also for their wills to be strengthened. Their wills are like rudders that will determine the direction of their lives. Every time they will to say "no" to temptation, they are directing their lives into God's will and plans for them.

As our children grow up, they will enter the minefield of high school or college or work and all the temptations of the world. It is then that we will better understand how vital it was to have made sure of their foundations while they were children. Life is a battleground, and just as no general in his right mind would send his soldiers into battle without appropriate weapons, so we need to make sure our children are spiritually healthy and armed with the appropriate spiritual weapons—the Holy Spirit and the Word of God.

In warfare, the weak ones soon fall and become a burden to the healthy troops, and it is the same in spiritual warfare. The weak and vulnerable ones fall prey to Satan and consequently divert the attention off the main battle. Thank God it's possible for our children to remain strong and gain the victory over temptation, but it won't happen if we leave it to the organized church to do it for us. Our children are *our* disciples, and we must battle for them until they are strong enough, and prepared enough, to send out on their own.

5

Coping With Rejection

*He was despised and rejected by men, a man
of sorrows, and familiar with suffering. Like one
from whom men hide their faces he was despised,
and we esteemed him not.*

(Isaiah 53:3)

Rejection is one of the greatest difficulties
experienced by Christians. Most families have a history
of rejection in preceding generations, and most of us
have experienced rejection in our own lives to one
degree or another. Rejection manifests in many ways,
and it always leaves us with poor self-esteem. We can
become angry, rebellious, resist discipline and authority,
seek revenge and not appear to have a low self-image;
or, alternatively, we can become withdrawn, introverted,
suffer from self pity, apathy, depression and wear low
self-esteem and unworthiness in an obvious way. The
end product of the first can be violence and murder,
and the end product of the second can be deep
depression and suicide.

Are you a person who is ruled by rejection, or have you learned to be an overcomer? Whichever you are, your children will most likely be, too.

Jesus

Let's first consider Jesus. The Bible says, "He was despised and rejected by men, a man of sorrows, and familiar with suffering. . . . He was oppressed and afflicted, yet he did not open his mouth; he was led like a lamb to the slaughter, and as a sheep before her shearers is silent, so he did not open his mouth" Isaiah 53:3, 7).

Jesus was despised and rejected by all, yet there was none of the justification, resentment, anger, or self pity that is the normal reaction of someone who is rejected—in fact, His reaction was just the opposite. He looked down on His mockers, accusers, torturers, and murderers that were gathered around the foot of the Cross, and then looked up and said, "Father, forgive them, for they do not know what they are doing" (Luke 23:34). Jesus' response to what they did to Him was not one of resentment and anger, but one of love—a love that not only forgave their sin towards Him, but even interceded for them before His Father.

Jesus knew the reasons why the people rejected Him as their Messiah, rejecting Him even to the point of crucifying Him. He knew what was in their hearts, their anxieties and fears, their self-concerns and motives—He understood all their weaknesses. He even understood that in rejecting Him as Messiah and crucifying Him, they thought they were doing the will of God. So He responded not out of anger, but out of knowledge, wisdom, and compassion. Because he was not consumed by his own rejection and feelings, Jesus clearly saw that these people really didn't know that they were killing the Son of God, and that they were rejecting God's love given to them in Him.

Responding to rejection in resentment, anger, hurt feelings, and the myriad of other emotions rejection can create as our pride reacts, is a sin. By not keeping it at arm's length, we become consumed with negative and self-centered emotions and attitudes. That's where Satan gains his edge. Jesus was rejected many times during His short ministry. But because His response to it was never sinful, there was no sin in Him. Satan had nothing in Him, no access to Him, and could not manipulate his emotions in any way.

You see, once we take rejection on board—that is, into our thoughts and emotions—it wants to be fed. It's like one of those little pac-men in the video games. It needs something to gobble up. It needs to be fed with more rejection. So, whenever anything is said to a rejected person, their spirit of rejection will cause a reaction of rejection, even when there is absolutely no rejection intended. Once a person gets to that stage, it is virtually impossible not to cause a response of rejection in them, no matter how careful you are around them.

Some people suffer enormous rejection early in their lives from such things as attempted abortion while still in the womb, loss of both parents, and abuse or neglect. Others suffer minimal rejection that occurs in any normal family situation where parents are unaware of the need to pray over seemingly unimportant situations.

Roots of Rejection

Thankfully, I grew up in a very secure family, and never had fears that my parents would split up, or that they didn't love me. My father was a gentle man who found it difficult to express his emotions, but I knew that he loved me. In retrospect, however, I realize that I didn't feel *unconditional* love and acceptance from him. He was very absorbed in his work, and when he wasn't working, he played golf. This made me fertile ground for the enemy to come into my life and plant rejection. Some forty years later, after becoming a Christian and having prayer for the foundations in my life, the Holy Spirit revealed to me the roots of what had become a flourishing tree of rejection.

During prayer, I recalled a incident that occurred when I was a little girl and accompanied my Dad to a nearby country town. He met up with several of his farming friends, and for what seemed to me like ages they talked about lamb prices, weather, and cattle. I was impatient and bored as I stood next to my father's trouser legs. When the gathering finally broke up, I trotted off with the trouser legs beside me. We had only gone a short ways, however, when I looked up and discovered that it was the wrong pair of trouser legs—the man was a total stranger. I can still remember the frightening feelings of panic and abandonment at the thought that my father had gone home without me and left me with a stranger.

Now this wasn't a major incident, and not a situation of parental neglect, but the Holy Spirit showed me that it was the root of much rejection in my life. I realized that I had actually spent my life trying to please my Dad in order to win his love. I had a desperate need to have his approval. I even learned to play golf. The major choices I made in my life as a teenager and a young woman were unconsciously directed towards gaining his approval. In fact, it was the attitude to my rejection—the idolization of my father, and later my brother, my boy friends, and ultimately my husband—that needed repentance, forgiveness, healing, and release. I came to realize that Jesus wanted first place in my life, and when I gave it to Him, the striving to please left me, and I had a new freedom in my relationships.

If you were to imagine my life as a tree, you would see a relatively healthy tree. But it was a tree with some slight damage and stunted growth. The damage caused a definite leaning in the wrong direction, which became a more acute angle the older I became.

Our children are young trees. We'll see them grow into strong, straight, healthy saplings, if we ask the Holy Spirit to show us where they need healing, strengthening, and correction.

Signs of Rejection

If we ask the Holy Spirit to show us signs of rejection in our babies and children, we will recognize them, and can ask Him to bring healing. In their book, *Evicting Demonic Intruders,* Noel & Phyl Gibson listed a number of symptoms of rejection in children and babies.

1. A baby may reject the mother by refusing to breast feed.

2. A child does not show love or respond to being loved. Affection may be resisted.

3. A child is rebellious or disobedient and resists discipline.

4. A child is quick to get angry, often with little obvious cause.

5. A child shows anxiety over little things, and is fearful of being left alone.

6. A child is insecure, and lacks self-confidence, and is always looking for acceptance.

7. Adopted children often display these symptoms:

    a) Fear

    b) A lack of identity. "Who am I?"

    c) Rebellion and anger

    d) Skepticism when told they are loved. They constantly look for acceptance.[12]

Inherited Rejection

Additionally, your children could well be hampered by rejection as part of their inheritance, handed on to them by their parents, grandparents, or great grandparents. Some babies are unwanted—even if only initially. An abortion may have been attempted during pregnancy. There may have been hospitalization, a separation from parents, a difficult birth, divorced parents. Parents may have been undemonstrative or absent. The middle child, with competition from siblings, can sometimes feel rejected, as can a child with exceptionally gifted, intelligent, or disabled siblings.

All of these things can cause rejection and have a snowball effect. A child who starts school while suffering from rejection is an obvious target for either rebellious behavior, or poor self-esteem that could result in victimization. Unthinking comments by teachers and teasing schoolmates only make the situation worse. Often such children will get to the stage where they can't receive love or acceptance from anyone, and are seemingly locked behind a wall of rebellion or low self-esteem. At that point they have, in fact, developed hard hearts and need Jesus to come and heal them. They also need to understand what has been happening, and need to learn to be overcomers.

Every child with inherited rejection, or who has been rejected by circumstances beyond that child's control, certainly needs prayer. If you're dealing with a baby or very young child, it will only be necessary to pray for the binding, breaking, and evicting of inherited spirits, and for healing. A baby will have no understanding of rejection, and will not have developed deeply ingrained habit patterns. However, if children are old enough to cooperate in prayer, and are starting to understand that they're having problems, they need to learn how they can become overcomers.

Explaining the concept of rejection to children is a difficult task. So here is an example of how it was handled recently.

I was asked to pray for a nine-year-old boy from a large family. He had hereditary spirits of rejection and Freemasonry, and had additionally received rejection from being in a family where his mother and father had little individual time for him because of the number of children. As a result, the boy had become withdrawn and apathetic. He had very low self-esteem. He thought his brothers and sisters were more popular at school, more accomplished at schoolwork, and more loved by his parents. He was in a vicious spiral heading deeper and deeper into rejection. He had asked for help, which is an important step. God always comes through strongly if a person is desperate enough to ask.

I talked to him about rejection. Most children don't even know what the word means, and we have to be careful to use words that they do understand. It's a good idea, especially when talking to a child whose self-esteem is low, to check their understanding of what we say. Otherwise, we can lose them, and they don't have the confidence to tell us that they have no idea what we're talking about.

Initially, of course, there was a need to pray for hereditary rejection. Ideally, in a situation like this, it's best for both parents to continue praying for strengthening of the child. Having dealt with the root causes, there then needs to be a lot of work done in breaking down the child's established behavior patterns, and also in what the family, teachers, and friends have grown to accept as normal behavior for this child. With this boy, it was important to get him to understand that he was actually attracting rejection. In other words, he was his own worst enemy, and consequently his brothers, sisters, and classmates seemed to get great pleasure in teasing him.

I tried to get across to him the concept of not taking on rejection. I asked him to suppose that someone had given him some bad prawns—he said he hated prawns. If he ate them, they would make him ill. If he left them on the plate, they had no power to hurt him at all, and couldn't affect his feelings. So it is what people said to him that made him feel bad about himself, useless, or no good at games or schoolwork. In other words, I explained, he felt rejected. It's by letting things get hold of him, like eating the bad prawns, that causes the hurt.

I told him how much the Lord loves him, and suggested to him that he write Jesus a letter every night, pouring out to Him his hurts, disappointments, and failings, and asking for forgiveness, healing, and help. He wrote his first letter that night and enjoyed doing it.

Last time I had contact with him, he was doing well, but he has an uphill battle on his hands. It's hard enough for a child like that to change, but for everyone around him to recognize that he has changed, which is part of the healing process, seems to be harder still. Once other children find a victim, its difficult to turn the situation around, and it's a difficulty that needs much ongoing prayer, spiritual warfare, and lots of love and affirmation by his family and school teachers. Nothing is ever too difficult for God, but it would certainly have been much better for this child had his ungodly inheritance been released by prayer before he was born, or at least soon afterwards.

Battling Rejection

Rejection is something that I've battled against long and hard, not only in myself, but in our family, and with many people I've prayed for. It seems as though everyone has suffered rejection to some degree. The key to healing is God's unfailing, unconditional, unending, and amazing love. One of the key Scriptures in the battle is 2 Corinthians 12:9, "But He [the Lord] said to me, "My grace is sufficient for you." This can be applied and amplified for personal use, and for the use of others, in several ways. Here are some examples:

The Lord's grace is enough for me.

He can meet all my needs.

He can meet my emotional needs.

He can satisfy every need I have—emotional, physical, financial, and spiritual.

I imagine myself a cup that He can fill to the very top with everything I need.

All I need to do is to ask Him to continually fill my cup.

Every other relationship or good situation in my life is a plus on top of my full cup.

If the Lord's love is sufficient, I don't need any other relationship in my life in order to survive. (We do need relationships in our lives, but we mustn't use them to fill *all* our needs. No person can fill *all* our needs, and if we expect them to do so, we will drain them and still not be satisfied ourselves.)

I only need His love and my cup is full.

Every other relationship in my life—my husband, children, family, and friends—are pluses, glorious pluses, but not essential to make my cup full.

All these relationships are the "overflowing" of my cup, and as such, have a glorious freedom to ebb and flow, not altering my cup because it is already full, and is being kept that way.

This verse has a liberating effect. It enables us to come into a fuller awareness of God's love for us, and consequently for others. It can set us free of any unfilled great hunger to be loved that we may have had as a child and as a young person, and enable us to love without conditions, because we can love out of a full cup that never needs to run dry. There will be times, of course, when we'll go under, and our cup will seem to be draining, but we have the key and the constant infilling of the Holy Spirit. Consequently, we can joyously proclaim that it's true: "If the Son sets you free, you will be free indeed" (John 8.36).

Staying Wounded

The degree to which we remain in a wounded state with an untended hurt, will be the degree to which we will be unable to give of ourselves and love others. In other words, the untended hurt will have the effect of limiting our ability to love others freely. If we are using the large amount of emotional energy it takes to nurture a hurt, we have much less love to give. To love freely is to love as Jesus loved—unconditionally, without thought of self or reward.

All of this is important to us, but it is vastly more important to our children, and we must constantly be on the alert to help them to rid themselves early of the wounds of rejection and not carry them into their adulthood.

It's essential that we teach our children how to obtain victory over such things by using *instant prayers*— that is, praying immediately about the problem before the hurt and subsequent negative emotions have time to become deeply embedded in them. The longer those negative emotions stay, the harder and longer is the road back to spiritual health. It's like the way it is with physical health. The longer they're ill in bed, the longer is the convalescent period, and the road back to health and full strength. Untended wounds, whether they be emotional or physical, will not go away if ignored, and will be difficult to get rid of if too much time passes between the wound and the treatment.

In his excellent book, *How to Survive an Attack,* Roberts Liardon writes:

> There is one great rule we must always remember: wounds left unattended attract evil spirits. In the natural, whenever an animal is badly wounded, vultures follow it, circle it, and when the animal is down, they attack and eat their prey. These dumb and skimpy birds did nothing to cause the downfall of their prey; they just take advantage of it and help it die. The same is true in the spirit realm. When a hurt or wound is left unattended, in any area of our lives, it attracts the enemy. He will follow you, circle you and aggravate you, until that hurt causes your downfall. If it is not dealt with, he will "feed" upon it until you are consumed.[13]

If we learn these lessons and exercise them in our lives for our children to see, they will learn quickly how to appropriate them in their own lives. They will have the advantage over most of us in that they will learn the lessons early, and will be skilled, disciplined, and alert soldiers, ready for the front line of battle early in their Christian walk.

Emotional Health

Young people who have learned to overcome rejection in their lives will be emotionally healthy. They will have learned that the Lord is the one who brings the peace that the world cannot give, and that He is the one who satisfies every person's deep need to be unconditionally loved. Consequently, they will not constantly be on the lookout for a mate in the anticipation that when they find that mate, they will finally feel loved. They will be able to live in the freedom and peace that Jesus promised—with their cup full, understanding that if and when they do marry, their cup will over flow.

The measure to which we walk free of rejection and, consequently, in greater freedom and emotional wholeness, will be the measure to which we can walk in power, authority, and victory over the enemy. The younger we teach our children this lesson—by instructions and by the example of our own lives, the earlier they will mature in all the fullness God has for them.

6

The Power of Love

*This is how God showed his love among us:
He sent his one and only Son into the world that
we might live through him.*

*This is love: Not that we loved God, but that
He loved us and sent his Son as an atoning sacrifice
for our sins.*

*Dear friends, since God so loved us, we also
ought to love one another.*

(1 John 4:9-11)

If there is one dominant theme in the whole of the
Bible, it is love. How God could love us so much is
impossible to understand, but He does. The Bible is a
love story from beginning to end—a love story of God,
the creator of all things, reaching out to us with a never
ending pursuit of love. No one is exempt from it no matter
how great their sin may be. God's love reaches out to
every person on this earth.

Love, therefore, is the greatest force; the most
powerful tool; the most complex quality, and at the same

time the most simple; the most healing, motivating, and glorious of all created things. Created, because without God there is no life and no love. God is love, and love is reflected in every facet of God's character. So it follows that we need to love above all else.

Loving Our Children

If we're to love our children and teach them in turn to love, we need first to be plugged in to the source of love, the Lord Himself. Our inability to love with God's love is the primary reason for difficulties in our relationships with our children. We are all born with a desire to be loved. God put it there—in us and in our children, and we are to be the physical demonstration here on earth of God's love for our children, who are also *His* children. Finding it difficult to love a God she could not see, a little girl said, "Why can't I have God with skin on?" When it comes to demonstrating God's love to our children, we're the ones with the skin on.

How pure our love is for our children, and how well we demonstrate that love, will determine how spiritual and emotionally straight and tall our children will grow. In his book, *How to Really Love Your Child,*[14] Dr. Ross Campbell details three vital things to help our children find love and emotional wholeness:

> The necessity of physical touch.
> Eye to eye contact.
> Focused attention.

Loving Duncan

Our family learned hard lessons about love from the time of the birth of Duncan. Six months after he was born, the first arrows of fear about his development started lodging in my heart. We weren't Christians. We had no idea about God's love or the battle of the evil one for our son. We were swamped in a raging sea of fear, despair, hopelessness, anger, pride, and panic. Doctors said things like, "Put him in an institution and forget about him, and have some more children," and, "He'll never be able to lead an independent life," and, the cruelest cut of all, "Your son is mentally retarded, probably severely."

Where was the God of love I'd learned about at Sunday School? How could He let this happen to an innocent child? How could He know how we felt? Whose fault was it? Our whole world seemed to have gone mad.

We faced it as best we could. We were determined not to "put him away," but how were we going to handle all the problems? Most of our friends backed away from us. They couldn't cope. I didn't blame them. I could barely cope myself. Since my husband, Michael, was away a lot, the burden of Duncan's care was mainly on me, and several of our friends told me they thought I was marvelous, and that they couldn't do it. I believed them and lived on my pride. I was doing something my friends thought was marvelous! I was strong! I was capable! I was amazing!

But I wasn't really. They couldn't see on the inside. They couldn't see the fear, the anger, the despair. In desperation, I cried out to God, "Okay, if you're real, I'll do it your way. If you're real, show me. You're the only thing I haven't tried. I'm desperate!"

89

God loves prayers of the heart—desperate prayers. The language isn't important, only the heart-cry. He heard my heart, He came, and He's never left. He turned life around completely. He showed me how to love Duncan who, up to this point, was unlovable. The only time I had really loved him since he was about eight months old was when he was asleep, lying innocently with his eyelashes curled up on his soft cheeks, looking peaceful and normal. Then he was lovable. But God gradually changed all that. He did a miracle in my life.

Over a period of time, God showed me how to love Duncan as He loves him, and Duncan changed—we all changed. He changed Duncan from someone who unknowingly sought to control and destroy our lives—physically, emotionally, and mentally—into who he is today: a young man full of love, joy, and peace. He doesn't seem to know the meaning of rejection, he's pure love and joy and we all love him now just as he is—that's the change God made in us. Sure, Duncan's frustrating sometimes, and he finds it hard to entertain himself, but in his spirit he's free, he's happy, he's love.

It wasn't just love that changed Duncan, of course, it was also God's amazing healing power, but it was love first and foremost. Sometimes I wonder who changed most, Duncan or me. I went on a search about Jesus' healing miracles. Did He really heal when He walked this earth? Does He still heal? Is He really "the same yesterday and today and forever"? (Hebrews 13:8). I took Duncan to a Christian healing services where they prayed for his deliverance and healing. Then God lead me to a wonderful, wise, and Holy Spirit-filled couple, Noel and Phyl Gibson. They prayed for Duncan right through his inheritance—Freemasonry, witchcraft, rejection, lust, pride, unbelief, birth difficulties, rejection. Gradually he began to change, to improve.

No, Duncan's body isn't healed yet, he still doesn't talk, doesn't concentrate for long periods, and he's a bit uncoordinated, but his spirit surely is different. He's strongly attracted to the things of God. He prays. Whenever he needs anything, he lets us know he wants someone to pray for him—and somehow he seems to know when other people need prayer. He's full of love, peace, and joy, and we love him more than we could have ever imagined.

When Cam was eleven, he told someone, "We had to have Duncan to learn how to love properly." The wisdom of children! I've learned so many hard lessons about patience, endurance, perseverance, self control, kindness, faith, hope—but most of all, love. No longer is there envy of *normal* children, and we've all discovered that instead of a stone to bear, we've been given a pearl to share.

God Uses Duncan

The Lord started changing lives through Duncan. The first was Penny, who is the same age as Duncan. When they first met, she was a beautiful little girl, about nine or ten—today she's a beautiful young woman. Penny wore her hair in bunches. She was a bit frightened of Duncan when she came to the house to play with Maggie, because he used to pull her bunches, and so she always gave him a wide berth.

Then one day we noticed that things had changed. Penny wasn't avoiding Duncan. She started sitting with him and singing him songs, and he, in turn, started following her around and stopped pulling her hair. We didn't ask her what had happened—the situation seemed too precious and fragile. Then one day she said, "I want to ask Jesus into my life, like Maggie has. I know now that He's real and that He answers prayers."

"How do you know that, Penny?" I asked.

"Well, you told me that He loves everyone—right?"

"Yes," I said, "that's right, He does."

"Well, if He loves everyone, that means He loves Duncan just as much as He loves me. Right?"

"Right!" I said.

"So I asked Jesus to show me how to love Duncan. And He did. And I do!"

So *that* was what happened! There it is again, you see, the power of love, working in the most amazing way. Penny went on to give her life to Jesus "just like Maggie had," because the Lord answered her prayer about loving Duncan.

Because of Penny, I've encouraged our children and other children to ask the Lord to show them how to love people they don't particularly like. Our children would sometimes come home from school and tell something about someone they didn't like, and I would say, "Well, maybe that person is really unhappy, and that's why they behave like that," or, "Maybe that teacher has a really hard life." At first they would tease and say, "There goes Mum again, making excuses for everyone". But gradually they started doing it themselves, and they started discerning what people's problems really were. They learned to love the person and not their behavior—the same way God loves. That's teaching our children to love. That's teaching our children to have the heart of Jesus.

The Power of Unconditional Love

Another life that Duncan touched through love is Toby. Toby has Downs Syndrome and is the same age as Duncan. When they were ten, they attended the same school. During that time, Toby developed a mysterious problem with his leg and decided that he couldn't walk, so he crawled everywhere. His parents took him to specialists and had him checked, but no one could find anything wrong with his leg.

This went on for months and his muscles starting to waste. Then his mother took him to swimming lessons and slipped by the pool and broke her leg. The school where Duncan and Toby attended had residential facilities, and it so happened that at the time of this accident, Duncan was staying temporarily for a couple of nights. To help Toby's mother, the matron in charge of the residence suggested to Toby's parents that he stay overnight with Duncan. She told of how excited Duncan was to have his friend to "show around." But Toby was still crawling on the floor, and he kept lagging behind.

For a while, Duncan got down on the floor with Toby—as if to see the problem from Toby's perspective, but apparently he got tired of that. So he stood up, took Toby by the hands, and pulled him to his feet. For the rest of the day he held Toby's hand, and Toby walked for the first time in months. We were all amazed that Duncan could do what even the specialists could not. Why could he do it? Because he loved Toby and was so happy to be with him. Probably most people in Toby's life at that time wanted him to be different, but Duncan loved him unconditionally. He just wanted to be with him because he was his friend. There it is again—the power of love!

Forgiveness and Love

Some years ago, the mother of two brothers, aged seven and nine, came to see me. She told me that their seven-year-old, whom we'll call Paul, was continually persecuting his older brother, whom we'll call Peter—and always getting in trouble and destroying his property, such as cutting up his clothes and smashing his watch with a hammer. His parents were worried and concerned that if the behavior continued, they would be facing dangerous problems in a few years. I agreed. I asked to see the younger boy, Paul, alone. Gradually I gained his confidence, and he told me that he wasn't the one causing all the trouble. "My brother does all these things himself," he said, "and blames me. I get so sick of telling Dad and Mom it's not me. They don't believe me, so I just own up and take the punishment. It's easier that way. My brother hates me, and he wants to make himself look good!"

For some reason, I believed him. And since he knew Jesus, I talked to him about the power of love and forgiveness. Paul agreed to try, with the Lord's help, to love his brother. We joined in praying a prayer of forgiveness, and he appealed to Jesus with all his heart for help—it was another one of those desperate prayers that God answers.

During the following week, Paul telephoned a couple of times, and seemed to be doing well. He still took the blame, but he kept on loving and forgiving his brother.

Toward the end of the week, his brother, Peter, sent me a note, saying, "Can I please come and talk to you and can you please make it soon?"

"Soon" was the next day, and Peter came with his mother and asked if we could speak in private. Amazingly, he confessed that Paul had never done anything to him, that he had deceived his parents into believing his younger brother was to blame when, in fact, he was the one who had done everything.

Now this young man *had* to confess, and this was the reason, in his own words, "I can't stand the love of my brother any longer. I feel guilty after all I've done to him."

And so the younger brother was vindicated, not by accusation, threat, or punishment, but by the power of love and forgiveness. Both brothers were then in a place where they could receive the love and blessing from the Lord. As King David testified, "The sacrifices of God are a broken spirit; a broken and contrite heart, O God, you will not despise" (Psalm 51:17).

We must teach our children that in order to walk the ways of God, they must walk the paths of love and forgiveness. Anything less is not acceptable.

Children are like sponges. They soak up love to the full, and if they don't have love, they become dry and shrink and waste away. We've all seen pictures and read articles of children in institutions without love. They really do waste away. We can't give our children too much love—too many material possessions, yes—but not too much love. If we concentrate on love, seemingly insurmountable problems have a way of sorting themselves out—if not right away, then eventually.

Proper Priorities

A wise pediatrician once told us to be careful about the things we decided to make an issue of with our children. She said, "If it's not harming the child, if it's not harming property, and if it's not harming or causing disrespect to other people, then maybe it's not worth making a big issue out of it." Those words are a very good guide in matters of discipline. If we save our energy and discipline for the important things, and spend ourselves in love, we'll find a better balance.

For example, it's sometimes better not to make an issue out of teenagers' clothes, hairstyles or the state of their rooms, but rather to look at the attitude behind the actions, or lack of them. It might just be an expression of peer pressure, but it might be rebellion coming from rejection. If we can keep the lines of communication constantly open with our children, we'll soon know what's troubling them, and we, with the Lord's guidance, can help them deal with it.

Some fathers say, "I'll spend time with my children when they're old enough to have an interesting conversation with me." Some mothers say, "My teenage daughter is going through a stage where she doesn't want to talk to me. It's normal. she'll grow out of it." Both have a deficit in their relationships with their children.

It doesn't have to be that way. If we spend ourselves in love for our children and concentrate on building a solid foundation for our relationship with them, with God at the center, then lots of other things—like hairstyles and clothes and messy rooms—will sort themselves out in time. In other words, make the relationship the issue, make sure the child feels valued, loved, and precious no matter what. Then there will be a solid basis upon which to tackle the issues that concern us as parents.

In addition, we need to be constantly in that state of communication with the Lord where we are saying to Him:

How do I handle this one?
What should my attitude be in this situation?
Please Lord, give me Your love for my child, and your perspective in this situation.

We need to pray Penny's prayer, "Show me how to love this child." Then, with God's help, we can discipline in love.

Mothers who don't work outside the home, or have an office in the home, are particularly blessed to be the parent who spends the most time with a new baby and with little children. Our society has sadly tended to look down on mothers who make a full-time "career" out of mothering, but it's a special privilege, and one that shouldn't be missed if at all possible. There are times when we're exhausted, frazzled, and at the end of ourselves, but, hopefully, most of us have learned that we don't have to wait until we get to church, or have our "quiet time with God" to receive His help. Those times are vitally important, but we need to draw on God on the spot. We need to ask the Holy Spirit to fill us with love, peace, kindness, self control, faithfulness, joy, strength— then we'll have enough. Our cups will be full once more, and we can give out to our little ones from that never-ending source of God within us.

So often we mothers have our priorities back to front. Our first priority must always be God. That doesn't mean we ignore the needs of our children, but if we constantly draw on the Lord for our cup to be full, we can give more of ourselves in love and patience. We'll find too that we'll have the Lord's perspective—remember Martha and Mary. Some things just don't need the time we spend on them, and with the Lord's perspective we'll learn what's important to Him.

Often it takes a long time to learn these lessons. When Duncan was small, one of the few ways to keep him happy was to go on walks. At first I resented the large amount time it took from the day, and having to organize the other two children to play with friends while we walked. There was also enormous frustration at having to leave unattended all the numerous domestic tasks that needed to be done. In looking back, however, I realize how much was learned on those long and frustrating walks.

For one thing, I learned to talk continually to God. Duncan was happiest setting the pace and walking ahead. He couldn't hold a conversation with me because he couldn't talk, but the Lord could. Slowly I realized the little joys of being able to walk, to smell the flowers, watch the birds, and pray for Duncan. At home, I slowly changed my priorities, stopped being so house-proud, learned cleaning short cuts, and became more like Mary and less like Martha. I also learned that when I'm weak, Jesus is indeed strong, and began to learn how to love as Jesus loves.

Honor and Respect

Honor and respect are components of love. God said "Honor your father and your mother, so that you may live long in the land the LORD your God is giving you" (Exodus 20:12). As parents, we have the opportunity to encourage our children to "honor" their father and their mother. This is a priceless gift that you can give to your children—and to your partner—and it will also provide God the opportunity to bless your children with long life.

When we've been hurt by our partner, we need to guard against the temptation to speak in bitterness and anger about him or her to our children. I remember being sorely tempted in this area, and I could so easily have turned the children against their father. At times when our children were young, my husband, Michael, would be away all week, and arrive home on weekends with a bag of dirty washing, and a weekend full of work commitments outside the home. My attitude about this in front of our children was critical to their relationship with their father. Would I answer their questions of "When is Daddy going to be home?" with a bitter "Daddy's too busy to spend time with us," or with a father-honoring "Daddy has an important job, and he'll be home as soon as he possibly can." If we have a problem, and take it to Jesus and deal with it, then our children won't have a problem, and they will be able to honor and respect their parents.

We need to look for opportunities with our children when we can build up honor and respect for our partners. This will have the effect of blessing our children. They will feel secure and at peace in their spirits and in their emotions as they hear us speak in this honoring way about our partners—and thus our families will be blessed.

7

The Perfect Family

So I went down to the potter's house, and I saw him working at the wheel.

But the pot he was shaping from the clay was marred in his hands; so the potter formed it into another pot, shaping it as seemed best to him.

Then the word of the LORD came to me:

"O house of Israel, can I not do with you as this potter does?" declares the LORD. "Like clay in the hand of the potter, so are you in my hand, O house of Israel.

(Jeremiah 18:3-6)

From the very beginning of my Christian experience, the picture of the "perfect family" seemed something totally beyond grasp, but also something incredibly desirable. Wasn't this the way we were supposed to be, the perfect Christian family—dad, mom, and two or three cutely dressed children? Such families were always shown on television, in magazines, in advertisements, on the front of publications, eating out, playing in the park, being perfectly happy together. So I tried very hard to present this picture, and to pretend that's the way it was. But it was an illusion.

From the time Duncan was about eight months old, it was impossible to leave him easily—not because I didn't want to leave him, but because not many people could cope with him. We made one desperate attempt at going to church when he was about a year old. I told the women in the nursery they would have to come and get me if he cried. "Oh no," they assured me. "We've coped with crying babies before. You just forget about him and leave him to us." Ten minutes later their anxious faces appeared at the side door. Could I come? They were sorry. They couldn't cope. We didn't go back for five years.

After much heartache and bitterness, I learned that it was impossible to maintain a picture of a perfect family. Not only was there Duncan, who made it totally impossible, but my husband has a job that takes him interstate and overseas frequently, and even when he is home, he is required to be out working most evenings and weekends. For a long time, I fought it. I complained, and nagged, and spoiled the infrequent times we did have—and Duncan spoiled them even more. We couldn't even take him out for a hamburger, he would cause such a scene. If we left him at home with a baby-sitter and took the other two children out, we would be burdened with guilt because he knew that he was different and that we sometimes left him out of family activities. We had one attempt at the perfect family holiday—camping. It was a complete disaster and we came home after two days.

After reading lots of wonderful Christian books on how to make it work but it never did, I gave up and threw myself on the mercy of God. Doing that brought forth the most wonderful discovery. *The perfect family is the fruit!* Before you have fruit, you have to have a healthy tree. And before you can have a tree, you have to plant seed in good, well-watered, drained soil—and there has to be a good root structure, strong branches, and healthy shoots. Wanting the fruit without planting the seed for a healthy tree, was approaching the problem the wrong way around.

The solution was to concentrate on what we had, on the individual relationships within the family, and stop looking at the ultimate and perfect family picture. I didn't change my attitude because of any thought that it was the right thing to do, but because it was the only thing that could be done. Looking back now that all the children all adults, it's obvious that it was God leading the way all the time.

Even if our family had been near perfect, we should have concentrated on feeding and nurturing the tree and tending it as it grew rather than going out and buying some perfect and socially acceptable fruit to display. Concentrating on building individual relationships with each family member, resulted in my having the most wonderful relationship with each of our children. That's the fruit! The picture the world sees doesn't matter any more, it's our individual relationships before God that count, and as they increasingly develop, so does the perfect family in the spiritual realm.

Special Times

One of the wonderful things God did for me when I first came to know Christ was to inspire the members of our church to offer to take Duncan off my hands for one hour every day. I didn't even pray for it. The Lord just did it as an act of compassion and love. It was the first time that anyone had offered to look after Duncan out of love. It was such a wonderful, generous, spontaneously amazing thing to do that at first I didn't know how to respond. But it gave me the opportunity to have what was to be known in our family as "special time" with our other two children.

For some time I had been worried that the amount of time and energy required to look after Duncan was having a bad effect on the other two children. I even got to the point of locking Duncan in his room for short periods—an action he heartily disapproved of—in order to just sit down and read a story, cook a cake, or kick a ball with the other two. This wonderful, generous, gesture by the members of our church provided the much needed opportunity of having that "special time" without the all consuming occupation of Duncan. In our family "special time" came to mean:

> this period of time is for you and me to spend doing exactly what you would like to do (this had limits and several suggestions from which the children could choose, such as going to the park, cooking, reading, painting, shopping, visiting);
> this period of time is my gift to you of my time, my love, my attention, because I value you and want to be with you, doing what you want to do, and not what I want to do.

These special times saved our family from disintegration at a vital point in our lives. It taught us an immense lesson. It was the beginning of that building of a unique relationship with each of the children. It taught the children that when they had something to share or ask or just talk over, they would have the opportunity to do that. It taught them to recognize the need in any close relationship to share on a deep level, and the necessity to plan and allocate time for that. It taught them to wait for that time, and to recognize that we were in need of time alone. Often they would vocalize it, "Mummy, when can we have some special time alone. I need it." It also taught them to recognize that their father and I needed special time alone, also, and they respected that.

As they grew older, I would occasionally take them out of infants and primary school for a day, just to have a day alone with each of them. When it was explained to their teachers the reason for the requested day off, they were always encouraging. We had great times going on ferry rides and trips to the zoo, and sometimes just quiet days at home. Although never easy to arrange, especially when both parents work outside the home, and life is so busy, it's worth planning and great to have *special time* treats to look forward to.

Story Times

Reading books together is also a great way to strengthen a relationship. Reading the Bible is, of course, essential, and there are many wonderful Christian children's books available. It's also good to read other things as well, and not concentrate only on Christian books. Both Maggie and Cam, however, always seemed to prefer stories that we made up. Maggie's favorite ones concerned animals, especially horses, and we had one long standing serial about a family of mice who lived in the school down the road. It got so complicated in the end that the children had to prompt me with all the names and what had happened in the story the previous night.

Cam's "imaginary" was usually about motor bikes, and he had a friend called Tom who was actually a koala who rode a motor bike. They had some hair-raising journeys at night—even tunneling through to China once, and always getting home just in time to fall asleep and be "woken up" by Mom in the morning.

The thing that puzzled me about these stories was that the children frequently begged to be the hero. When the morality was raised, "You have to understand that you won't always be the hero, or the best at things you do, in real life," they would say that if they won in the "imaginaries," then it wouldn't matter if they didn't win in real life. Although I've never been completely comfortable about that explanation, it hasn't seemed to harm them. These imaginary stories were a good opportunity to weave in little moral values, which often seemed to hit home, even if unconsciously on the children's part.

Relationships

The point of all this is to emphasize the special relationship that began to be built up and nurtured with each child. Duncan needed lots of special and exhausting attention, of course, but gradually all the family developed a new love for him. So slowly, with special times and imaginaries, we built up our individual relationship with each other. By so doing, we put down the roots of our family tree, built strong branches and shoots, and are now seeing the fruit. It's no longer important what sort of *family picture* we're presenting to others. There's a freedom when we stop pretending and trying to make it happen. There's a freedom for God to work in our family and to do His work when we stop pretending we're coping, and stop trying to present a together image. Our family was like that pot in Jeremiah 18:3-6, "the pot He was shaping from the clay was marred in His hands; so the Potter formed it into another pot, shaping it as seemed best to Him."

When we submit our lives and the lives of our families to the Master Potter, no matter what sort of a broken mess we might be in, he can form us into another pot, one that seems best to Him, and only He knows what is best for us. There were times when it felt as though our family was in a furnace; but it's like Job, who was tested and said, "But He knows the way that I take; when He has tested me, I will come forth as gold" (Job 23:10).

That promise can be for us and for our families if we pick it up and hold it before God. Take your broken pot to the Master Potter—you could not be in safer, more gentle, more loving, more powerful, or more creative Hands. And then stand still and see what He will do. Trust him—He will never fail you.

8

Learning the Hard Lesson of Relinquishment

I tell you the truth, unless a kernel of wheat falls to the ground and dies, it remains only a single seed. But if it dies, it produces many seeds.

(John 12:24)

In parenting, all the difficulties and struggles of relinquishing everything to God are brought fully to light. We might think that we have relinquished the control of our own lives to the Lord, but when it comes to relinquishing the control of our children's lives to the Lord, we often come into deep inner conflict. As we watch our children grow and reach certain ages that bring back memories of our own childhood and youth, we will start living—or trying to relive—our lives through them if we're not careful. The unmet needs of our childhood, and the unfulfilled dreams of our youth, coupled with our awful pride, can start manifesting themselves and

109

cause us to manipulate the lives of our children. We desperately want them to be the best in everything—the cleverest, most popular, most talented, best behaved, best looking, and often without considering the cost to them, and to others.. Parenting seems to have the ability to show up our hidden unfulfilled desires and unmet needs in a most alarming way.

The deeply hidden ambitions and desires we hold for our children's future become nakedly obvious when our children are severely disabled. Like a search light, it shows up the bruised ego of a parent who has a child who never measures up to their expectations and who, as far as the world is concerned, appears to be a minus to society rather than a plus. In fact, a disabled child is, in some ways, a little like a death in itself—it's a death of the expectations of a normal life for that child.

Learning Relinquishment

One of the most painful lessons I've ever learned was to hear the heart of God through Duncan. Coupled with the difficult process of relinquishing him to the Lord, there was an equally difficult battle through accumulated years of anger, fear, despair, and hurt. Within me, pride had developed over the fact that I was actually coping in a situation that my friends and family found totally daunting, and meeting the enormous challenge that raising Duncan represented.

In the final process of relinquishing him, I quite clearly heard the Lord say, "Have you really relinquished him?"

Quite certain, I said "Yes, Lord."

He said, "Even if it means that I take him. Even if it means that he dies?"

As I struggled with the enormity of that, and cried an instinctive, "Oh, No Lord!" I felt this incredible wave of love and compassion from Him, but there was no compromise in what He was asking me to do. He said, "That is what I mean by relinquishment."

I was stunned, but I knew without a shadow of a doubt, that was what He meant. Relinquishment is death. It's not just letting go—it's killing it off. Now I understood what Jesus was talking about when He said that unless a kernel of wheat falls to the ground and dies it remains alone.

When our kernels of wheat—our dreams and desires for our children—fall and die, the Lord will produce a harvest that is so much better than anything we might have dreamed for our children. The apostle Paul wrote, "What you sow does not come to life unless it dies" (1 Corinthians 15:36). God established this principle when He told Abraham to put his precious son, Isaac, the promised seed of a whole nation, on the altar and kill him. Why would God want Abraham to kill the promised seed of His chosen people? It was in order for many seeds to be produced. As Abraham relinquished all rights to do it his way and trusted God with Isaac, God provided a substitute. As Abraham proved that his uppermost desire was for God's will in his life and the life of Isaac, then God provided the substitute sacrifice.

Practical Side of Relinquishment

Naturally, as we relinquish our children to God, we all want to know what this means in practical terms. Obviously, we are still responsible for our children. We have to provide shelter, food, clothes, education, direction, spiritual training, and love for them. What has changed, however, is the attitude of our heart. That is the most important element. We make a decision to do it the Lord's way, relinquish the rights to all final decisions, and trust Him completely. Although nothing great seems to happen at first, as we progress further down the road we can look back and see all the changes that have taken place as a result of our heart-decision.

The main difference for me was that when I let go of striving, pushing, manipulating, and controlling the lives of our children, I found myself standing by and watching each one of them develop in the most surprising and delightful ways. They weren't the ways that were planned for them before I relinquished them, but the ways of God were so much better in every way for each of them. My main task has been to encourage them in their walk with God, teach and guide them, and love and nurture them. In it all, I've had the most incredible sense of freedom. It was marvelously freeing not to be in control. It's been like watching some unique creation gradually unfolding before my eyes.

Jesus said, "Which of you, if his son asks for bread, will give him a stone? Or if he asks for a fish, will give him a snake? If you, then, though you are evil, know how to give good gifts to your children, how much more will your Father in heaven give good gifts to those who ask him!" (Matthew 7:9-11). Surely herein lies the heart of the matter. When we give gifts to our children, even though the gifts may be good, our motives are usually evil because we are evil, and unconsciously we are probably giving the gifts to satisfy our own egos or desires, or to promote them for what we think is their good, but is really for our pride. God, however, gives them good gifts that are specifically for *their* good, and He has no ulterior motives for doing so. And He knows exactly what they need. Our Father in heaven is all-knowing, all-loving, all-powerful and all-wise. We are none of these things. As we increasingly trust Him with the decisions concerning our children, we will see with wonder and awe His perfect will unfold for them, and see in perspective how selfish and limiting would have been our plans for them. We always need to remind ourselves that they're His children as much or more so than ours. Could His plans for them, therefore, be anything but perfect and good?

Sometimes, however, things seem to be going horribly wrong. A child may have a terrible disappointment, a loss, an emotional deprivation, an illness, an accident, or a disability, and we feel as if God is not in control. In these situations we need to ask ourselves whether we have done all for which *we* are responsible, such as having used every avenue of prayer and taken advantage of the medical help that is available. During all this, our attitude of relinquishment must be saying, "Lord, we've done everything for which we are responsible. If there's more we should do, then please show us. This child is Yours. We trust You and thank You for the answer."

Whatever we're going through, we must remember that the Lord can bring good out of a seemingly impossible situation (Romans 8:28), if only we'll give Him the opportunity through relinquishment. When we've done all that, we stand on the promises, then watch our wonderful God work. He won't let us down. He

113

can't—even though it may seem so for a while as though He has. But He never does, because He loves this child of ours *much more* than we can.

Controlling Our Children

In the stories of mothers in the Bible, we can see the same struggles as we've all felt in ourselves. Women seem to be particularly vulnerable to the temptation to manipulate and control situations, even if it's very subtle. We see it first in Eve who decided for herself that she would eat the forbidden fruit. She doesn't consult Adam, she doesn't go and check with God, she just decides for herself, and takes control of the situation.

We see it in Sarah who can't see any way in which God's promise of a son for Abraham could be fulfilled through her. Instead of trusting in a seemingly impossible situation, she decides upon a plan that will make the promise happen. In other words, she will help God fulfill His promise by giving her maid to her husband so that they will have the promised child. As she discovered, God doesn't need that kind of help from us. The child she organized with her husband and her maid Hagar, was Ishmael, who became the head of the Arab nations, which today are still living out the words of the angel of the Lord to Hagar concerning Ishmael, "his hand will be against everyone and everyone's hand against him, and he will live in hostility toward all his brothers" (Genesis 16:12).

We even see the same attitude of attempting to fulfill the destiny of God in Mary, the mother of Jesus. Mary knows the destiny of Jesus, and she must have been eager for that to be recognized among her people. She must have been eager for Him to start His ministry. After all she had lived with this incredible vision for Jesus for thirty years, and must have wondered when it would be fulfilled. We see it first at the wedding at Cana when the wine runs out. Mary goes to Jesus and tells Him, obviously expecting Him to do something about it, but He says: "Dear woman, why do you involve me? My time has not yet come" (John 2:4).

Again, when Jesus was casting out demons in a house overflowing with people, Mary and His brothers were concerned about Him: "When his family heard about this, they went to take charge of him, for they said, 'He is out of his mind'" (Mark 3:21). They don't understand and are fearful, and they want Him to stop and come out to them. They send someone to call Him and He sends back the chilling message, "Who are my mother and brothers?" (Mark 3:33). He can't allow Himself to be called away from doing His Father's business by His mother and brothers who think "He is out of His mind." He must carry out His commission exactly as His Father directs Him, and He can't allow Himself to be dissuaded by His earthly family.

My heart has always ached for Mary over verse thirty-three. I see now that Jesus could not allow Mary or His brothers to interfere because they didn't understand what He was doing. They needed to relinquish their ideas about the way He carried out the work He had to do. We need to do the same concerning the work God has for our children to do.

When our children are old enough to make their own decisions, and we have taught them to hear from God, then we must let them do what they believe is right. Mary was in danger of trying to direct Jesus' ministry, admittedly with good motives, and Jesus ignored her pleas. The next we hear of her in the gospels is at the Cross, where Jesus acknowledges her as His mother and asks John to care for her.

Peter also tried to dissuade Jesus from walking in His destiny. When Jesus predicted His death to His disciples, Peter rebuked Him with "Never, Lord. This shall never happen to you!" (Matthew 16:22). Jesus knew that it was Satan influencing Peter's words, and said to Peter, "Get behind me, Satan! You are a stumbling block to me; you do not have in mind the things of God, but the things of men" (Matthew 16:23).

We need to recognize the temptations to interfere with the destiny of our children. Our main aim should be to ensure that they know and hear clearly the voice of the Lord when He speaks to them. That should be the point at which our direction in their lives should be aimed. Once they reach that point, we need to take our hands off their spiritual guidance, unless they ask for our help, and continue only our prayers for them.

Teaching Relinquishment to Our Children

Of course we also need to teach this lesson of relinquishment to our children. It's so easy if we start early, for the first big relinquishment they have to make is always the hardest. After that, they know the victory and the freedom it brings, and they will have less struggle with the big things because they've learned with the little things. Is your child developing a passion for something? It might be a sport, a particular interest or hobby, or it could be a relationship with someone. There always seems to be some activity, or some person, that early in life nearly consumes all of a child's attention and interest.

When this happened with Maggie and Cam, I encouraged them to give the activities back to God. With Maggie it was horse riding, and with Cam it was snow skiing and surfing, and later it was music. They were both given these questions to ask themselves: "Is this passion from the Lord, or is it something I am using to fill a need in my life that only God can fill? Is it something that brings me closer to God, or does it take me away from Him?"

For both of them it took quite a long soul search, and eventually they had to ask themselves the questions: "If God wants to take this desire away from me, can I give Him permission? Can I live without this thing I like?" They both struggled with the answers, but eventually relinquished the things to God—and in each case, God hasn't taken away the gift or skill, but somehow the passion is different. They know they can live without it, and there's great freedom in that. They know that their desires are God's desires, and out of this they also know that it is *them* that God loves, and not any special abilities they may have.

God wants us to enjoy the abilities and possessions He has given us, but He doesn't want them to possess our hearts. Our hearts must remain His. Nothing must ever get in the way of God. He must be our first passion. When He is, all things fall into their proper order and perspective. "Do not love the world or anything in the world," John the apostle wrote. "The world and it's desires pass away, but the man who does the will of God lives forever" (1 John 2:15, 17).

Relinquishing Health

As I write this, Cam has just recovered from a three year illness in his last years of school. After we had prayed long and often, followed medical advice, and done all we could responsibly do, Cam decided to relinquish his right to good health. It wasn't a glib thing to do, it was very hard, but it seemed to him the only thing left to do. In effect he said, "Lord, if you want me to have this illness for the rest of my life, then that's okay—it's your life anyway." There didn't seem to be any immediate change, but there was a change of attitude. It's hard to describe, but it seemed that instead of the illness ruling his life, it assumed a different perspective. In fact, his attitude toward illness now is something strangely and wonderfully different—as if he's been through the valley of affliction, and it can't ever touch him in the same way again. That doesn't mean that he won't ever be ill again, its just that his attitude is different. Perhaps this is something of what Jesus meant when He said, "whoever loses his life for me will find it" (Matthew 16:25).

Dying to Things

If children can learn to do this with the small things, it will be much easier and less painful when it comes to relationships, especially with the opposite sex. If children have learned that they can trust God, then it will naturally follow that they will trust Him to show them their future partners in life. They won't waste time and emotional energy trying to work out who they will marry, or even if they will marry at all. They will trust God to bring that person into their lives at the right time, and they can get on with enjoying their friends.

Losing our lives is letting go, relinquishing, dying to the things we think we have a right to have. Jesus says that if we want to save our lives we will lose them anyway, so our attitude must be one of letting go and relinquishing our lives to God—then we will know the freedom and peace that Jesus came to give.

Our Will for His Will

There are so many wonderful facets in our relationship to God. Relinquishment of our wills for our lives to His will for our lives is one of them, but it doesn't mean that we then disregard spiritual warfare, standing firm in faith, seeking prayer from others, and exercising the other spiritual disciplines. There are times when we really need to battle against the powers of darkness, particularly with regard to illness, and we need to exercise strong and determined faith and persistence. Relinquishment doesn't mean developing an attitude of give up, don't try, and leave it all to God. Nevertheless, the sovereignty of God is supreme, and we need to submit to His will in all things.

119

9

God Has No Grandchildren

Jesus answered, "I tell you the truth, no one can enter the kingdom of God unless he is born of water and the Spirit.

Flesh gives birth to flesh, but the Spirit gives birth to spirit.

You should not be surprised at my saying, 'You must be born again.'"

(John 3:5-7)

Jesus is specific when he talks to Nicodemus about a new birth—a birth of the Spirit. He says that we must have this birth of the Spirit if we are to enter the kingdom of God.

As parents, we are responsible for helping our children take this step of being "born again" in the Spirit. We must never assume that because we've talked to them about God since they were born, and prayed with them— and they can talk Christian talk—that they're automatically spiritually born again. God has no grandchildren—just because we've been born again, doesn't mean our children have, also. They must make that decision, individually, for themselves.

Leading Children to Jesus

Recently I was asked to pray with a young daughter of a minister about some problems she was having at school. When I asked her if she had ever asked Jesus into her heart, she said she had not, but she really wanted to even though everyone assumed she had. I encouraged her to speak to the Lord herself, and it was a wonderful time for her.

She said that for the first time she really felt special in God's eyes. She also became quite excited when I told her that because Jesus is King of kings, and she is His daughter, then she is a princess—a princess of the Most High King. I gave her a diary, and the last I heard she was writing to Jesus every day. Later, she sent me a card that said, "To Robin: Thank you very much for your talk. I am a happy princess with God. I just can't get over how happy I have been."

When you do lead your children to Jesus, make a special note of the date. Maybe you could buy them their own personal Bible and write the date in it. That way, nobody can take from them the decision they've made, and it won't be possible for them to wonder, years later, if they actually have been born again. Sometimes, children ask Jesus to be their Savior at such an early age, they can never remember not knowing Him, but it's very important that you remember and tell them about it.

The words a child speaks to the Lord for salvation aren't as important as the intention of the heart, but here are some phrases you could use for small children.

Dear Jesus, I know that you made the whole world and everything in it. That means You made me too. Thank you for dying on the cross so I could know you. I'm sorry for all the wrong, bad and silly things I've done, and for the good things I haven't done. Please forgive me. Please make me one of your special children. Please come and live in my heart for ever.

Another little girl that made that special decision and was born again, simply stood on the sidewalk as we walked toward her home one night, and spontaneously raised her arms in the air, looked up toward heaven, and said, "Jesus, come into my heart!" And He surely came. Her heart was open and eager, and that's all God really needs—the words are never as important as the attitude of the heart.

Jesus delights in little children—they are always close to His heart. Introducing your children to the King of kings will be the most important introduction you'll ever have the honor of making. Please don't miss it!

10

Children of the New Covenant

*The time is coming, declares the LORD, when
I will make a new covenant with the house of Israel
and with the house of Judah.*

*It will not be like the covenant I made with
their forefathers when I took them by the hand to
lead them out of Egypt, because they broke my
covenant, though I was a husband to them, declares
the LORD.*

*This is the covenant I will make with the house
of Israel after that time, declares the LORD. I will
put my law in their minds and write it on their
hearts. I will be their God, and they will be my
people.*

*No longer will a man teach his neighbor, or
a man his brother, saying, "Know the LORD,"
because they will all know me, from the least of
them to the greatest, declares the LORD. For I will
forgive their wickedness and will remember their
sins no more.*

(Jeremiah 31:31-34)

125

There are seven major Covenants written about in the Old Testament between God and His people, Israel, and the one in Jeremiah is the seventh—the New Covenant, which would be established by Jesus on the Cross on Calvary. It's an unconditional divine promise to unfaithful Israel to forgive her sins and establish God's relationship with her on a new basis by writing His law "on their hearts." It's a covenant of pure grace, a covenant of promise, and the promise of the Holy Spirit for all God's people, not only for the natural branches, but also for the grafted branches (Romans 11:17-24). This is the promise that all people will not only know *about* God but will *know* God.

This covenant promise was made as Israel was about to be exiled because of her unfaithfulness and idolatry, and is the promise of a God still yearning for and loving His people, despite their betrayal of Him. It contains the promise of forgiveness of sins that Jesus bought for all people on the Cross.

The word *covenant* is not generally used today. We have contracts and promises that are broken, often quite light-heartedly broken, but the concept of a covenant that is binding and cannot be broken is not a modern day concept. Even marriage vows for some are lightly taken. There always seems to be an out with most vows and contracts. The covenants God makes, however, are unbreakable and irrevocable—and whatever covenant promise God makes, God keeps.

David and Jonathan

There is a story in the 9th chapter of second Samuel that represents God's covenant faithfulness. David and

Jonathan, the son of King Saul, made a blood covenant long before David was king (1 Samuel 18:3-4). After the death of Saul and Jonathan, David, who is now king, knows that the covenant he made with Jonathan is still in effect because a covenant applies to every one of the dead person's children who are still living. David therefore institutes a search for any family members of Jonathan's that are still alive, so that he can carry out the covenant he made with Jonathan.

> *David asked* [his advisers], *"Is there anyone still left of the house of Saul to whom I can show kindness* [marginal reference: "covenant faithfulness," NKJV] *for Jonathan's sake?"*
>
> *Now there was a servant of Saul's household named Ziba. They called him to appear before David, and the king said to him, "Are you Ziba?"*
> *"Your servant," he replied.*
>
> *"Is there no one still left of the house of Saul to whom I can show God's kindness?" Ziba answered the king, "There is still a son of Jonathan; he is crippled in both feet."*
>
> *"Where is he?" the king asked. Ziba answered, "He is at the house of Makir son of Ammiel in Lo Debar."*
>
> (2 Samuel 9:1-4)

David then has Mephibosheth brought to him so he can fulfill the "covenant faithfulness" conditions of the covenant he made with Jonathan. When Mephibosheth arrives, David says to him, "Don't be afraid, for I will surely show you kindness for the sake of your father Jonathan. I will restore to you all the land that belonged to your grandfather Saul, and you will always eat at my table" (2 Samuel 9:7).

Surely this story represents the covenant Jesus made for us with God. Because He is in covenant with God, and because we are in Him, God gives us all the spiritual blessings that belong to Christ, and has us feast at His spiritual table, no matter how unworthy we appear. Jesus Himself said, "And I confer on you a kingdom, just as my Father conferred one on me, so that you may eat and drink at my table in my kingdom" (Luke 22:29-30). This promise is not only for now, but also for that great banquet in heaven when the last days are fulfilled.

Let us rejoice and be glad and give him glory! For the wedding of the Lamb has come, and his bride has made herself ready.

Fine linen, bright and clean, was given her to wear." [Fine linen stands for the righteous acts of the saints.]

Then the angel said to me, "Write: 'Blessed are those who are invited to the wedding supper of the Lamb!'" And he added, *"These are the true words of God."*

(Revelation 19:7-9)

Urgency of the Last Days

As we get closer to the day when Christ returns, the Church is being increasingly refined to make us ready to take our role as His eternal bride. There is an excitement and urgency in His Body as this refining accelerates, and there is a heightened awareness of the need of holiness

128

and of increasing the work of fulfilling the great commission.

Our children are a part of this urgency. Those who have received Christ are being refined to a more intense degree than has been the case in the past. The enemy is also on the march. He senses the urgency, and increasingly is seeking to defile the hearts, minds, and bodies of our young people.

Our children who have been born again are children of the New Covenant. They are "a chosen people, a royal priesthood, a holy nation, a people belonging to God, that you [they] may declare the praises of Him who called you [them] out of darkness into His wonderful light" (1 Peter 2:9).

In these dark times, our children need to be equipped as never before. They don't have a leisurely span of time in which to learn the things of God; so it is while they're still young that they should start learning what God has called them to do. We can help them with our prayers, undergirding, encouragement, teaching, wisdom, and understanding as the Holy Spirit prepares them to be part of God's great end-time army.

It's essential that we parents sense the urgency of the times, and assume the responsibility of discipling our children before they are snatched and ensnared by the evil one.

This is the Word of the LORD for parents today:

Fix these words of mine in your hearts and minds; tie them as symbols on your hands and bind them on your foreheads. Teach them to your children, talking about them when you sit at home and when you walk along the road, when you lie down and when you get up. Write them on the doorframes of your houses and on your gates, so that your days and the days of your children may be many in the land that the LORD swore to give your forefathers, as many as the days that the heavens are above the earth.

(Deuteronomy 11:18-20)

and teaching them to obey everything I have commanded you. And surely I am with you always, to the very end of the age.

(Matthew 28:20)

As Christians, let us not fail our children in our responsibilities toward God.

As parents, let us not fail God in our responsibilities toward our children.

Notes

[1] *Getting the Best Out of The Bible - A New look at Biblical Meditation* by Selwyn Hughes, Copyright 1989 by Selwyn Hughes, (CWR, Waverley Abbey House, Farnham, Surrey GU9 8EP, England).

[2] *Christianity With A Human Face* by Ranald Macaulay and Jerram Barrs, Copyright 1978 by Ranald Macauley and Jerram Barrs, (InterVarsity Press, P.O. Box 1400, Downers Grove, IL 60515, USA).

[3] *Free Indeed,* by Tom Marshall, Copyright 1975, 1983 by Orama Christian Fellowship, (Sovereign World Ltd,, PO Box 777, Tonbridge, Kent TN119XT, England).

[4] *Blessing and Curse - You Can Choose!* by Derek Prince, Copyright 1990 by Derek Prince, (Word Publishing, Milton Keynes, England).

[5] Psalm 139: 23-24

[6] *Deliver Our Children from the Evil One* by Noel and Phyl Gibson, Copyright 1989 by Noel and Phyl Gibson, (Freedom in Christ Ministries Trust, Drummoyne, NSW Australia).

[7] *The Secret Life of the Unborn Child* by Thomas Verny M.D. and John Kelly, Copyright 1981 by Thomas Verny M.D. and John Kelly, (Warner Books, Division of Little Brown & Co. UK Ltd., Brettenham House, Lancaster Place, London, England).

[8] *"Stop, Look & Listen"* by John Fox, Copyright 1977 by John Fox. Used by permission of Australian Broadcasting Commission Music Publishing, ABC, GPO Box 487, Sydney, NSW 2001, Australia.

[9] "Foreword" by Andy Butcher (Editor, Christian Family Magazine) from *How To Really Love Your Child,* Dr. Ross Campbell, Copyright 1977 by SP Publications Inc., (Victor Books, P.O. Box 1835, Wheaton, IL USA). Used by permission of Chariot Victor Publishing.

[10] *The House of the Lord* by Francis Frangipane, Copyright 1991 by Francis Frangipane, (Word (UK) Ltd, 9 Holdon Avenue, Bletchley, Milton Keynes Mk 11 QR, England).

[11] Ibid.

[12] *Evicting Demonic Intruders* by Noel & Phyl Gibson, Copyright 1993 by Noel & Phyl Gibson, (New Wine Press, Chichester, West Sussex, England).

[13] *How to Survive an Attack* by Roberts Liardon, Copyright 1954, 91 by Roberts Liardon Ministries, (Embassy Publishing, Laguna Hills, CA 92654, USA).

[14] *How to Really Love Your Child* by Dr Ross Campbell, Copyright 1977 by SP Publications Inc., (Victor Books, P.O. Box 1835, Wheaton, IL USA).